I Remember Paducah When...

by

BARRON WHITE

McClanahan
Publishing House

International Standard Book Number 0-913383 72 4
Library of Congress Catalog Card Number   00-108771

Second Printing, December, 2002

Cover design and book layout by James Asher Graphics

Manufactured in the United States of America

All book order correspondence should be addressed to:

Barron White
4704 Buckner Lane
Paducah, KY 42001

(270) 443-1205
ebwhitey@yahoo.com

McClanahan
Publishing House

DEDICATION

This book is dedicated to the memory of my parents,
Edna LaFreniere and Egbert Barton White;
my sisters, Ruth and Edna;
and my wife, Zelma, along with our daughters, Kathy and Liz.

ACKNOWLEDGEMENTS

This book could not have been written without the support of so many people. My sincere thanks to all of those who encouraged me to write and who helped to make this effort possible.

I wish to express special thanks to certain contributors. Those who furnished pictures: W. W. Dyer, Jimmie Curtis, Jack Johnston, Charley Cissell, Mary Ellen Rutter, Joe Le Beouf's daughter, Dean Hauter, and Carver Rudolf. Thanks to Vonnie Shelton of the Paducah Library; Bob Petter and Ruth Gurd, who told me about Krispy Kreme; and to W.L. Beasley who shared his experience of book publishing.

Also I want to recognize the suggestions and encouragement of daughters Kathy and Liz and nieces Bette Dwinell, Joanne Litzsinger, and Beverly Martin. And thanks to my brother, Harry, who was supportive as always. A special thanks to my editor, Gay Baker and Paula Cunningham, my publisher, for their astute and valuable guidance and assistance throughout. Thanks also to Jim Asher for the book's design.

Lastly, my deepest thanks and appreciation to my dear wife, Zelma, for her patience and tolerance during the years when all she saw of me was the back of my head as I pounded out stories on my word processor. Her suggestions and final proof-reading were immensely helpful.

CONTENTS

FOREWORD

It was after I returned from three years in the U.S. Air Force and to my job at the Petter Supply Company that I began to write of my experiences in Paducah. I had no idea I would do so, but when I began to work with new employees and to tell them stories of how we worked before I left for the service, many commented that I should write a book.

Since high school days, I have been interested in taking pictures. During my working years I became acquainted with all the buildings in town - the industrial plants, churches, schools and many of the fine old homes. So whenever I learned that a landmark building was to be destroyed, I rushed over to take a picture. Over the span of many years, I have collected quite a few. It was only when I decided to retire in 1989 that I began to write. I joked with fellow employees, telling them that after I left the company I was going to write the "good, the bad and the ugly," about them. As a going-away gift they pitched in and gave me a check for several hundred dollars to buy a word processor and challenged me to get started.

When I began giving talks six years ago, I discovered, much to my surprise, that many people seemed interested in what I have written. Many told me that talking about old times in Paducah brought back their own memories of earlier days. They told stories that newcomers and young people did not know.

So many Paducahans are interested in our city's rich history, heritage and growth. During the years since my retirement, I have had the time and inclination to do quite a lot of research and the more information I find, the more fascinating it becomes.

As a Paducah Ambassadors volunteer for the past 10 years,

I have given verbal sketches of Paducah stories to visitors who come here from around the world on the riverboats and for conventions. The most frequent question they ask is, "Have you lived here all your life?"

I tell them, "Not yet."

How Paducah Grew
The 1800s to Present

*B*ack before 1830, the year Paducah was chartered, the population was a little over 100. By comparison, Smithland was the largest town in the extreme western part of the commonwealth with approximately 400 people. Salem had 250, Columbus around 200 and Mayfield had fewer than 50. So Paducah stood fourth in rank. But by the mid-1800s, Paducah's strategic location enabled it to become the largest city in the Jackson Purchase. By 1880, the population was more than 8,000 and 10 years later it had grown to 13,000. By the turn of the century, it had almost doubled to 23,000.

What caused this rapid growth within two decades? It must have been our manufacturing concerns, wholesale operations and excellent transportation capabilities. Access to the Ohio, Tennessee, Cumberland and Mississippi rivers, railroad connections, marketing activities and being right in the center of larger cities - St. Louis, Louisville, Nashville and Memphis - made Paducah the hub within a radius of 150 miles.

Let's take a look at Paducah in 1900. We had about 24 large companies in operation, making a wide assortment of products in good demand and use and a number of wholesalers furnishing supplies in a wide area to all the surrounding states. There was a general diversity of manufacturers here, 10 of which supplied wood and wood products. Two concerns made vinegar, two were tobacco processors and two were saddle and harness manufacturers. There were two boat supply stores, three wholesale grocers, three packet boat operators and about forty towboat companies. There also were three railroads, the Illinois Central (IC), Nashville, Chattanooga & St. Louis (NC& St.L) and the Chicago, Burlington & Quincy (CB&Q).

Very few firms in existence in 1900 were still in operation by the 1920s. The Wallace-Gregory Vinegar Works was one which was. It operated out of a four-story building right on the ICRR tracks at 11th Street and Kentucky Avenue. They had their own tank cars for transporting the raw juice from the mills to their plant. This company manufactured 78,000 barrels of vinegar a year. That much vinegar would fill 800 ordinary freight cars, requiring 40 trains to transport them. Some 21 salesmen traveled territories far and wide. Where did that business go? Why Paducah did not retain it, I would like to know.

By 1900, Paducah boasted the largest concentration of lumber and wood-related products on the inland waterways. There were large plants all the way from the Clark's River-Island Creek area to Washington Street. Many companies were phased out soon after automobiles replaced horse-drawn vehicles. But there was still a large demand for lumber and finished millwork. There are very few today with the capability of sawing, milling and finishing wood products.

Despite the loss of all those companies, Paducah grew in population, which by 1930 had increased to 34,000. This growth continued, but at a slower pace, except for the boom when the atomic plant was built in 1950. This plant caused Paducah's population to balloon to about 45,000 for a brief period during construction. It peaked at around 36,000 in the mid-'70s. Today Paducah has a population of approximately 26,000. A big part of the decline was caused by a migration into the county, which has grown from 30,000 in 1900 to a combined city and county figure of 60,000, at present.

Hello, Paducah

The Whites Come To Paducah

My father's family was from Greenfield, Tenn., a small town about 100 miles south of Paducah. My grandfather, James E. White, owned a grocery on Main Street. The railroad tracks of the Illinois Central main line from Chicago to New Orleans ran parallel to Main Street, right through the center of town.

Dad graduated from Bowling Green Business School, now Western Kentucky University, with a degree in accounting. He moved to Memphis and was office manager and bookkeeper for the Broadway Coal & Ice Company, a sales outlet for the West Kentucky Coal Company, which had offices in Paducah, which were managed by Ralph Vennum. In 1910, Dad married Edna LaFreniere and by the time they decided to move to Paducah in 1923, they had four children - two boys and two girls.

We came to Paducah by train, all loaded down with suitcases and two hat boxes. I don't remember if we had our furniture and household goods shipped to us. As a 10-year-old, I didn't bother about things like that. Nor do I remember how we got from Union Station to our new home. We probably rode the streetcar. If we had taken a taxi, I would remember, for we had never ridden in one before. We were just interested in getting here and exploring our new world.

Our family moved into the Napoleon Apartments, a two-story four-unit building that faced north on Washington Street near the corner of 4th Street, the present site of Vietnam monument in Dolly McNutt Plaza. Ruth, Harry and I were enrolled that fall in Robert E. Lee Grade School, which was at 4th and Ohio streets, within walking distance of home. Lee School was torn down years ago and at present is the location of the Duke & Long Oil Company, which will soon be re-located to the corner of 5th and Broadway. This was the former location of the J.C. Penney Company and before that of the wonderful old Palmer House Hotel.

All the Paducah schools we attended during our 12 years are now gone; most have been demolished and probably forgotten. Jefferson School (middle school) which was on the corner of 8th and Harrison, one of the very first Paducah school buildings, is gone. Washington Junior High on Broadway between 12th and 13th, which had been Paducah High School until 1921 when Augusta Tilghman was built, was torn down in 1965. The Augusta Tilghman building is now being remodeled into apartments.

We scouted around the neighborhood and soon met new friends and became fairly well adjusted to our new environment. We discovered Draughn's private school near the corner of 5th Street and found the McCracken County Courthouse one block north on 6th Street. We learned that downtown Broadway was only two blocks away, with five movie houses - the Arcade, Columbia, the Kozy, the Star and the Orpheum, all near the corner of 5th and Broadway.

The Elks Club and First Baptist Church were on 5th Street just across from the Orpheum. The Palmer House Hotel on the corner had a drugstore, as did many of the downtown Broadway corners. Oehlschlaeger's Drugstore was on the northwest corner of 6th and Broadway and Dad's new grocery was at 621 Broadway, now Bradshaw & Weil Insurance Company.

We didn't own a car and didn't need one. Any and everything we wanted or needed was within a few minutes walking distance. We considered "downtown" an area from Washington Street to Jefferson and from 7th Street east to the Ohio River. After a few years, we knew almost everyone in the stores, schools and churches and the residents of most of the downtown homes. If we needed to go anywhere very far from home we took streetcars. Paducah had 17 miles of streetcar track, which ran to all parts of town - South Third, 6th, Guthrie Avenue, Murrell Boulevard, Union Station, Wallace Park, the Fairgrounds (now Carson Park), Broadway, Jefferson and Oak Grove Cemetery. In the 1920s, the street railway system was owned by the Kentucky Utilities Company which also owned the electric power system. There were a number of taxicab companies we could call for the rare occasions when we had to get somewhere in a hurry. The one I remember best was the 606 Cab, which used only Studebakers. It was next door to Dad's grocery and had the phone number 606.

There were nine full-service gas stations downtown - three on Kentucky Avenue at the corners of 4th, 5th and 6th streets. The others were on Broadway at 7th and 9th and on Jefferson at 4th, 5th, 6th and 10th. In 1931, gasoline sold as low as 15 cents a gallon. Attendants would come out as you drove up, pump your gas, wipe your windshield and check your oil, battery and tires. Some also gave stamps for dishes.

Beyond the downtown, west of 7th Street, south of Washington, north of Jefferson, was almost 100 percent residential except for corner grocers, filling stations, churches and schools. Most merchants owned their businesses and some lived upstairs over their businesses or close by.

Our First Move and New Neighborhood

My uncle Grady White came to live with us when we had been in the Napoleon apartment a little more than a year. We needed more room, so in 1924 we moved into the upstairs apartment in the James Langstaff's big frame home at 731 Kentucky Ave., which was back-to-back with the old George Langstaff family home on Broadway. The Langstaffs came to Paducah in the mid-1800s from Mt. Holly, New Jersey, and settled in an area of town they called "Jerseyville," now shown on maps as 3rd and Elizabeth streets. They acquired 30 acres of property with 2,000 feet of Tennessee River frontage and established the Langstaff-Orm Lumber Company. With its sawmills and storage yards, it was one of the largest sawmill and lumber operations in the country.

Fine old homes

We loved that neighborhood. Kentucky Avenue was a nice, pleasant and relatively quiet, mostly-residential neighborhood and we soon became acquainted with everyone who lived there. There were a number of fine old beautiful homes occupied by prominent Paducah families and a number of old landmark buildings which have long since been destroyed. One that comes to mind is the Guthrie-Wheeler house at 504 Kentucky Ave. It was built in the 1870s by John James Guthrie, a prominent merchant who operated Guthrie's clothing store on Broadway. His daughter, Mamie, married Charles K.Wheeler, maternal grandfather of the late James G. Wheeler, a prominent Paducah attorney.

Charles K. Wheeler represented the First Congressional District in the 55th, 56th and 57th congresses. The Market House

Guthrie-Wheeler House, 504 Kentucky Ave

Museum became the owner of Wheeler's congressional desk. While in Congress, Wheeler took a stand against paying Spain $20 million for ceding the Philippines to the United States. It was during this period that the Wheeler house was visited by William Jennings Bryan and Kentucky Governor William Goebel.

In later years, the house was used as a studio for radio station WKYB. The house was torn down in 1957, its iron work made into a gate at the Jefferson Street home of Charles K. Wheeler's son, James.

The Terrells

Richard G. Terrell, a wholesale grocer, lived at 516 Kentucky Ave., next door to the Guthrie-Wheeler home. The Terrell home was a beautiful house set back in the lot with a nice front yard and driveway. Terrell operated a business at North 2nd Street in the late 1800s, dealing in "Groceries, Salt, Hay, Cement and Agricultural Instruments." A number of Terrell family members lived in the big house.

Sid Terrell, a tax collector, had his office in the grocery on North 2nd Street. Fletcher, Fred and John Terrell operated the Terrell Brothers Livery Stable at 129 S. 4th St. Chiles and Tom Terrell worked in the family businesses. An earlier Sid Terrell, in 1835 was proprietor of the Terrell "Distillery #34, Paducah, Kentucky." Their brand name was "Old Terrell, a Sour Mash Whiskey Sold Direct from Distillery to Consumer to Rehandler."

Mrs. R.G. Terrell was still living in the home in the early 1900s. In the 1940s, Mrs. Mildred Terrell and Mrs. Frances T. Walker lived there. In 1963, the sole occupant was Mrs. Walker, who rented the garage to Curtis Young, an electrical contractor, for his office and storeroom. In the mid-1960s, the whole south side of the 500 block of Kentucky Avenue was cleared to make way for the new Paducah Public Library.

Richard G. Terrell Jr. and Horace P. Terrell operated the Terrell Floral Company, which for many years was located on the ground floor of the Palmer House, with a greenhouse at 300 Lovelaceville Road.

Terrell Apartments was on the northwest corner of 5th and Kentucky. This was a three-story 11-unit apartment building featuring a front verandah on each floor. Next door at 519 Kentucky was the home of Mrs. Mary Terrell. From the mid-'30s until the '50s, it was a house with "furnished rooms." For a while it was the location of the Loyal Order of Moose, then after many years of vacancy it was purchased by St. Francis deSales Catholic Church and is the present parish hall.

The Riekes

Another fine old home was the residence of Charles F. Rieke at 528 Court St., now Kentucky Avenue. It was a two-story frame house, surrounded by hedges on the southeast corner of 6th and Kentucky. In the early '20s, when we lived in the Napoleon Apartments around the corner at 5th and Washington, I passed the Rieke house every day on my way to my father's grocery at 621 Broadway. I knew Charles F. Rieke's daughter Carrie, who became a good friend of my parents.

Charles F. Rieke was owner of C.H. Rieke & Sons Company, "Wholesale Dry Goods & Notions," located at 110-112 N. 3rd St. Other firm members were C.L. and Louis M. Rieke. Others living at the home were W.M. Rieke, a partner in L.B. Ogilvie & Company, dealers in "Staple and Fine Dry Goods, Notions, Carpets & Oil Cloths," at 330-332 Broadway. Also at the home were Clara B. Rieke and Mrs. C.L Rieke, widow of Charles H. Rieke.

The Rieke family was prominent and involved in a number of enterprises in Paducah from the turn of the century in 1800 and during many of my young and adult years here. Among their kin in Paducah were Louis M. Rieke and Mrs. Mary Rieke, who lived at 703 Jefferson St. in a fine old red brick two-story house which was torn down many years ago. Louis married Faith Langstaff about the time I graduated from high school.

Frank Rieke, who lived on Fountain Avenue between Broadway and Jefferson, was a partner in the W.H. Rieke & Sons Company at 322-324 Broadway. Like the other Rieke companies it dealt in "Staple and Fine Dry Goods, Notions, Carpets & Oil Cloths." Frank also owned the Paducah Ice Company at 112 North 1st St. William H. Rieke and William H. Rieke Jr. lived at 531 Broadway and Mrs. Mary E. Rieke at 318 S. 6th St.

The Court Street Rieke home was torn down and the site became a Standard Oil station operated by John Decker. In the mid-'60s, it was one of the sites cleared for the Paducah Public Library. Kentucky Avenue as I remember it from the 1920s, has undergone a complete change from almost completely residential to commercial.

Barron, Edna, Ruth and Harry White, Langstaff home, 1925

The Langstaff Family

W hen in 1924 we moved into the upstairs apartment of the James Langstaff home at 731 Kentucky Ave., their family consisted of the father, James D. Langstaff, his wife Adine (Corbett), and their children James D. Jr., called "Pete," Ina Claire, Tommie, Morton and John. We were older than the Langstaff children, but enjoyed their companionship while we lived there.

We soon discovered that the big house on Broadway that was back-to-back to the one we lived in was the home of the George Langstaff family, the parents of our landlord. Although the Kentucky Avenue home was a big three-story frame house with a large yard, it was small compared to the Broadway family home which sat squarely in the middle of the block between 7th and 9th streets and had a very large yard with several hundred feet of frontage. At the time, George's other sons, Sam and George Jr., lived with their father in the Broadway home. George's sister, Faith, owned a home just to the west of the Broadway home. George died in 1944 at the age of 82. His wife, Ina Quigley Husbands Langstaff, preceded him in death in 1942.

James D. Langstaff died in 1948 at 62. He served in World War I with the 77th Infantry Division, which became known as the "Lost Battalion." Sam Langstaff and his wife, Elizabeth (Burch), were parents of Sam Husbands, Robert B. and Susan, who married William R. Bowman of Bluefield, W.V. Sam Sr. died in 1971 at 71. Faith Langstaff, who was head of the Kentucky Employment Service for 20 years, died in 1955. George Quigley Langstaff moved to Nashville, Tennessee, and continued in the lumber business after the closing of the Langstaff Lumber Company. He and his wife, Katherine Irion, were the parents of George Q. Jr., Witt and

Quintus A. Langstaff.

The Langstaff homes, built back-to-back, were spread over several lots on Kentucky Avenue and between 7th and 9th streets on Broadway. The James Langstaff home was a three-story frame structure, while the George Langstaff home was a two-story brick. The Broadway home was at the time one of the most famous residences in Paducah. It was built around 1850 by William and Ed Norton, partners in the Norton Brothers Bank which was in the St. Francis Hotel building at 1st and Broadway. George and Augusta Langstaff bought it in 1868 and the family continued to live there until the 1940s. Both Langstaff homes were demolished around 1949. The Kentucky Avenue site is now Rhew-Hendley Florist. The Broadway site became first a supermarket and is now the home of Comcast Cable.

In September of 1927, it was announced that a new 10-story hotel was to be erected on the Langstaff property at 800 Broadway. Nashville architects Marr & Holman drew the plans and R.E. Hyde, manager of the Hermitage Hotel in Nashville, was to be resident manager of the new hotel. The plans were to have 300 rooms, "each equipped with a bath," a banquet hall and ballroom to accommodate 200 diners, a private dining room, ladies' parlor and ladies' restroom. There would be three shops on the first floor facing Broadway. The hotel would have its own refrigeration and heating plants, barber shop, beauty parlor and billiard room. Three high-speed elevators would be installed. The hotel was never built. Had it been, the Irvin Cobb, built in 1929, might not have been a reality.

The Angles

In the mid-1800s, Mrs. George Langstaff's parents, Quintus Q.Quigley and Mary Husbands Quigley, discovered what they described as "the prettiest farm we have ever seen." It was "out in the country," and was comprised of about 50 acres in three separate parcels which angled at one juncture. They envisioned a house at the juncture where the three parcels met. The land cost $1,000. Quintus, a Paducah attorney, had saved $1,000 to buy a ring for his wife but they decided to use the money to buy the land. The house they built was called The Angles. They used it as a summer home and a place to entertain their grandchildren when they visited on weekends and summer holidays. It became a favorite hunting place for the grandchildren.

The Angles remained in the Langstaff family until 1938 when it was sold to then U.S. Senator Alben Barkley. In June of that year, all generations of the Langstaff family gathered on the lawn for a final picnic before turning the property over to the Barkleys. Fifty years later, in June of 1988, descendants of the family met again for a picnic at The Angles, which became the home of Dr. Jim and Anne Gwinn.

The Downtowner

On March 5, 1963, the "*Paducah Sun-Democrat*" featured a front page article about a proposal to build a five-story, 100-room Downtowner motel on the site of the 80-year-old R.G. Terrell house at 516 Kentucky Ave., which had 150 feet of frontage on Kentucky. Included in the plan were an underground parking level, 120-seat restaurant and heated swimming pool with a patio. The motel would feature exterior balconies. The article included a picture of the Downtowner Motor Inn in Nashville, Tennessee, "similar," it said to the one proposed for Paducah. The project would represent a $1,250,000 investment and would be one of a national chain of 11 other Downtowner motels reportedly under construction, with plans drawn for an additional 30.

The proposed Paducah property was described as "the last of a once imposing row of brick residences." It was to be acquired from Mrs. Frances T. Walker in a transaction by Paducah realtor Paul Bynum.

The motor inn was never built and no known records

explain the reason. A few years later, the whole block was acquired by the city for the new Paducah Public Library.

Sunset Beach

One summer Sunday afternoon in the mid-1920s, my father took the family to swim at the sandbar across the Ohio River from downtown Paducah. We took our bathing suits and six large towels, boarded the small shuttle boat at the foot of Broadway, bought a 50-cent round-trip ticket and rode over to the large strip of sand that stretched for over a half mile along the Illinois shore. We docked at the pier, read the rules posted at the gate and bought a 50-cent all-day ticket for each of us. We walked through the boathouse to the separate men's and women's locker rooms and changed into our swimsuits.

Swimming at Sunset Beach on Illinois side of Ohio River, 1920s

There were several wooden walkways parallel to the shoreline and one that extended out to the deep water beyond which signs warned swimmers not to go. Two lifeguards were on duty and made frequent use of their whistles when swimmers got too rowdy or failed to obey posted rules. Our parents were the only ones in our family who knew how to swim, so we children spent our time wading and playing in the shallow water no more than chin deep. We stayed until almost sundown and came home tired and happy.

The sandbar appeared for a few more summers, but after a number of locks and dams were built to raise the pool stage of the river, the sandbar became only a fond memory. I did not know the sandbar ever had a name until I retired and began researching Paducah history. I found a mention of it in Fred Neuman's book, *Story of Paducah*, and learned it was known as Sunset Beach. Neuman said although the beach had been there for a few years, it was not until 1921 that lockers and other conveniences were provided.

A Business
is Born

Dad Opens a Store of His Own

My father grew up working in his father's grocery store in Tennessee and must have always wanted a store of his own. So after working in Memphis as an accountant for 12 years, he opened his first store here in Paducah at 621 Broadway in a building owned by Saunders Fowler. The Fowlers were an old-time Paducah riverboat family and had operated a number of steamboats since the mid-1800s. Old Judge Fowler moved here from Smithland and raised five sons, Joe, Dick, Will, White and Gus. All became owners and pilots of steamboats. Joe was owner of the wharf boat at the foot of Broadway and family members operated a boat supply store at 1st and Broadway. There were many Fowler relatives living here when we arrived in Paducah and the old Joe Fowler home was still standing in the 700 block on Kentucky Avenue. Saunders Fowler's son, Gus, was a clerk in Dad's store before going off to college.

Paducah's first "cash & carry"

Dad's store was promoted as the first "cash & carry" grocery in Paducah. It was widely advertised and became a very popular and successful business. It eventually was expanded to stores at five locations - two on Broadway and one each at South 3rd, Jefferson and at 16th and Madison. The death of my father in 1933 at the depth of the Depression caused the business to be liquidated.

When the first store was opened, it carried the name United Thrift Store. Two years later, the then three stores operated under the Clarence Saunders franchise. During the last four years, the name was changed to White Food Stores.

Despite having only curbside parking in the early days, a

number of retail grocers did big business in the heart of the down-town business district. In addition to my father's stores on Broadway and South 3rd Street, Piggly Wiggly had a store next to the Columbia Theater, and on 4th and Jefferson, were the Rector's and Downen's stores. Meacham had a lot of stores around town with two on Kentucky at 2nd and 3rd streets. Lackey's was a few doors from the Market House.

Grand Opening, June 1923

Market House business

The Market House had 66 produce farmer and grower stalls and many farmers would back their wagons and trucks up to the curbs along Kentucky Avenue between 1st and 2nd streets every morning, hawking their wares until all their buyers were gone. Among the growers were the Rottgerings, Legeays, Schmidts, McCutcheons and the Bichons. Butcher stalls in the middle of the Market House were owned by the Metzgers, Rectors, Petters, Bullmers, Switzers and the Jones brothers, T.A. and R.O.

In addition to the downtown groceries, there were more than 100 small neighborhood "mom and pop" stores scattered all over town, usually located on corners. There were also a few larger grocers, some of whom delivered. Among them were the Sloan Brothers at 12th and Jefferson, Bennett Brothers at 2401 Broadway and Roof Brothers on South 7th Street.

There were a number of wholesale grocers who provided us and other retail stores with canned goods and staples. There were Covington Brothers at 4th and Jefferson, Clark-Lack Grocers across the street at 4th and Jefferson, M. Livingston at 11th and Kentucky and Bray Smith and Baker-Eccles near the Market House. Several food brokers maintained offices and warehouses in the market area.

Strawberries

Barger & Golightly, one of the big suppliers of produce, were also agents for the McCracken County Strawberry Growers Co-op. During their peak years in the 1930s, they shipped over 700 carloads of Dixie Aroma and Blakemore strawberries by rail to markets nationwide. This kept the Paducah Box & Basket Company on 11th and Caldwell in business making boxes and crates for the strawberries. Paducah Ice & Manufacturing built a plant along the railroad tracks near Union Station, primarily to supply ice for the strawberries. The Nagel Packing Company at 8th and Jones packed peaches and tomatoes and marketed them to local groceries.

M. Livingston roasted and packaged coffee at its 11th and Kentucky plant for sale to local and area markets

When farmers could no longer get laborers to hand-pick strawberries and other crops, the wonderful business of selling and shipping our crops to northern and eastern markets gradually faded into history and the strawberry association slowly folded. It took down with it several other prosperous businesses, including Paducah Box & Basket, and reduced the ice manufacturing market to only local needs and eventual demise.

Kirchoff Bakery on South 2nd and Burns & Vaughn on South 3rd were the biggest bakeries in town and operated fleets of trucks to make daily deliveries of bread, rolls and pastries to grocers all over town.

Several dairies supplied milk and daily products not only to grocers, but delivered door-to-door every weekday morning. The largest dairy was the City Consumers Company at 10th and Monroe, which sold its products under the Goldbloom trade name. It occupied the site and building that had been the Paducah Brewery Company, which was converted to dairy products when Prohibition was enacted in 1919. Dexter and Dudley dairies also distributed milk at the time. Paducah Ice Manufacturing and the Home Ice Company delivered ice door-to-door.

Competing for the business

I worked in all five of my father's stores during the 10 years they were in operation and I was well aware of the competition between our stores and the bigger ones. The most competitive stores ran weekly ads in the two Paducah newspapers, the morning *News-Democrat* and the *Paducah Evening Sun*. Bennett's Grocery was out of our downtown drawing area and catered to the more affluent west end of town. It specialized in fancy fruits and more expensive brands of canned goods. Sloan Brothers, owned by Mert and Sam Sloan, was a well-established company and made deliveries all over town. Meacham's store attracted the lion's share of the business from farmers, since it was only a block from the Market House. Roof Brothers had a lot of customers we hoped to attract. Until Piggly Wiggly came to town a year after we did, ours was the only "cash & carry."

We had been downtown a year when Grocer's Baking Company opened a bakery across the street, making bread and pastry products. In those days, all groceries had no or limited parking, so customers had to walk along the street and many walked from nearby residences.

Thrift comes to town

In 1923 my father opened a new style grocery in Paducah. He ran full-page ads in the newspapers announcing the grand opening on Saturday, July 26, 1923. The headlines read, "Thrift comes to town in a basket." Ads outlined special features of the new store, such as a monorail system for moving shopping baskets around the shelves, allowing for hands-free shopping (grocery carts had not been thought of yet). Air ducts fed a stream of air around the store doors to keep flies out. An attractive water fountain with changing colored lights was in the front window; it also provided moisture for the fruits and vegetables. This was before air-conditioning and automatic refrigeration, so the ice company came twice a week to replace ten 300-pound cakes of ice which were stored overhead in the walk-in meat case.

From the beginning, the new business attracted a big following. For the next 10 years, the company prospered and expanded to three stores, the number one store was moved to 10th and Broadway in a larger building with parking alongside. The number two store was moved from South 3rd Street out of the commercial area to 5th and Jefferson, a residential area. Store number three was opened at 16th and Madison in the middle of a neighborhood populated primarily by newcomers to Paducah who moved here to work for the new Illinois Central Railroad shops built on Kentucky Avenue in 1927, at a cost of $8 million and which became Paducah's biggest payroll, employing almost 1500 people.

The stock market crash of 1929 took its toll in Paducah.

Many shop people moved to Detroit to look for work in the auto plants there. Many of our regular store customers who could not pay cash for groceries, went to grocers who extended credit. As a result, the number three store was closed. In May of 1933, my father died of a heart attack and we were forced to sell the business.

Special Memories of Dad's Stores

Since Dad's first grocery was at 621 Broadway, only four blocks from our Napoleon Apartments residence, and was a "cash & carry," we did not deliver and did not need or have a car. But when store number one was moved to 10th and Broadway and two more stores were opened, we needed a vehicle to pick up produce at the market and deliver to all three. So a second-hand Model T Ford truck was purchased. It had a long bed with wire side panels and no doors. One of the clerks taught me to drive and use the three foot pedals for shifting gears, backing up and braking. I thought all cars had the same shift and when the Ford A models came out, I had to learn all over again.

My father often took me to the Market House as he selected supplies for the stores. We would get there at 4:30 in the morning and make the rounds, going first down the line at the curb, then making purchases within the Market House. When all purchases were made, we would load up the old Model T and deliver portions to each store before it opened at 6 a.m.

When we moved to North 25th Street, we got a 1923 Dodge sedan which doubled as a business vehicle and family car. When used for the grocery, the back seat was removed and replaced by a wooden platform to hold boxes of groceries and produce. Another wooden platform was made to fit on the front bumper to hold several more boxes. For after hours and Sunday use, the two platforms were removed and put in the garage so the back seat could be put back in. When my brother Harry and I were old enough to drive, we ran the wheels off that sedan, using it every weekend to transport our dates around town. After a full day's work, Dad was ready to rest and didn't care if we used the car.

A black family was hired to work part time and when the store was moved to 10th and Broadway, they moved into a small house on the alley behind the store and became full-time employees. In the lot behind the store, the mother helped her husband kill and dress chickens for the Saturday trade. There were two teenage sons who also helped and worked for other families in the neighborhood.

Oxford Hotel, NW Corner Fifth and Jefferson
The Oxford Hotel was a Paducah landmark for over 50 years. It was there in
1930 when my father opened his second store across the street. The hotel was built
in the early 1900s by the James E. Wilhelm family and was first known as The
Wilhelm. When Kate Craig became the proprietor in 1908, she changed the name
to The Craig. A week before her death in 1924, she sold the building to Sam
Hughes McKnight. It then became The Oxford and continued to operate until
January, 1966, when it closed and was demolished, a "victim of the national trend
against the traditional downtown hotel."

My father and uncle always called me, "Brother," and soon Leon Raper, the store manager; Glen Campbell, the assistant manager; and Clarence Liebel, the butcher, picked it up. It was, "Brother, get me a box," or "Brother, get some more sacks," and so on so I got used to it.

I first got to know Don Williams when he stopped by the 10th Street store just after 5 p.m. every weekday on his way home from work downtown to pick up the order Mrs. Williams had called in. I didn't know where he worked until I began working at Petter Supply and found he was Stanley Petter's right-hand man. We became good friends during the years we worked together in the office.

Roasting Coffee

The Bockmans were said to be one of the city's oldest and most well-known families. The head of the family, Eugene W. Bockman, was listed in the 1894 city directory. The family operated a grocery and coffee roasting plant on the southwest corner of 7th and Kentucky. Eugene was president, oldest son John, or J. Fred, as he was known, was vice president and son Henry was the coffee roaster. They advertised in the newspapers of the era and apparently had a thriving local business for years. Family members lived in several houses just west of the grocery.

Eugene died in 1916 and J. Fred succeeded him as president. Another brother, Joseph, entered the business and became the shipping clerk. When the United States entered the war in 1917, Henry, who was the only roaster, joined the Army. J. Fred then closed the business and went to work for the L.S. Dubois Drug Company as bookkeeper and continued there until the mid-1930s. While returning from a trip to St. Louis in February, 1936, his car skidded on an icy road near Chester, Ill., and he died a few years later of injuries he received in the accident. He was 42. His widow, Edna, died 11 years later. The only remaining member of the Bockman family is Barbara Bockman Holt, wife of Emmett Holt.

No known record explains why the flourishing Bockman business was closed. World War I may have been a factor and it also is thought they may have sold their business to another grocery and roasting business. Harry Livingston, son of Lee Livingston, one of the three Livingston partners in the M. Livingston Wholesale Grocery Company, formerly at 11th and Kentucky, suggests his forebears may have bought out the Bockmans.

The M. Livingston Company did a thriving coffee roasting business in the 1920s and 1930s. Their coffee beans were packaged in one-pound paper bags under the name Goldblum and was very popular in all local grocery stores. Most grocers had coffee grinders and would grind purchases while customers waited. At 10 every weekday morning, the delicious smell of roasted coffee permeated the downtown area.

The C.C. Cohen building, still on the southwest corner of 2nd and Broadway, was built originally to be the main office of the M. Livingston Company. The warehouse was directly across the street behind the old Sinnott Hotel. The company never occupied the new building, but loaned the second floor for Jewish religious services while a temple was under construction. Later, the warehouse was moved to North 1st Street near the corner of Jefferson, then later to the southeast corner of 11th and Kentucky in the building that had been occupied by the Wallace-Gregory Vinegar Company.

A Thriving Downtown

Living Downtown

There were still several old barns in the downtown block where we lived, most of which served as garages. All had haylofts and two were half filled with hay and still had that wonderful old smell. We neighborhood boys used the barns as play houses, much to the annoyance of the owners who were afraid we would get hurt. We roamed up and down the street, rummaging through everyone's backyards, and felt this area belonged to us as much as it did to the property owners.

Between the two Langstaff homes was an earthen mound about 20 feet in diameter with a hinged door leading to a cave below. An old rickety ladder led down to the inside which was always full of water, several feet from ground level. It was very dark and foreboding and we were warned never to go down into it. Rumor had it that the cave had been used in Civil War days to hide and smuggle slaves who were fleeing to the North. Years later, when the Langstaff homes were demolished to make way for a grocery on Broadway, the contractor dug the mound and failed to find the tunnel to the river some had thought existed.

We grew up with the children in the neighborhood, went to school with them and remained friends. I remember Custis, Tommie and Margaret Fletcher; Pete, Ina Claire and Tom Langstaff; Luke and Julian Nichol; Henry and Owen Cummings; Bill Mills; Bill Bugg; Billie Reeder; and Ed and Mildred Bringhurst.

Mrs. Bringhurst was a granddaughter of Joe Fowler. Another Fowler grandchild was Frank Davis, who lived in the Tilghman home. Frank and I used to visit the two Fowler sisters, Martha and Josephine, who were next door in the old homestead.

The historic old place was rundown with sagging floors that squeaked and groaned when you walked on them. The exterior was a dull gray and sadly in need of paint. Both ladies were elderly and did not get out much, but they maintained an air of quiet dignity and old-fashioned charm. Their property took up about half of the block on Kentucky with a large grape arbor in the back, which provided the neighborhood children a wonderful place to romp and play and fill up on grapes.

When we went downtown, we usually visited the dime stores or stopped at one of the many soda fountains in the drugstores. It seemed there was one on every Broadway corner. Oehlschlaeger's

Temple Israel, SW Corner Seventh and Broadway

was at 6th, Walker's and Gilbert-Bennett's at 5th and a second Gilbert-Bennett's and Segenfelter's at 4th. List Drugstore, between 4th and 5th, did not have a fountain, but had a Toledo scale up front. Almost everyone who walked by used it to check their weight. Wilson's Book Store, near the corner of 3rd Street, also had a fountain.

Movies

Among the first places we wanted to find were the movie houses. The center of downtown was at 5th and Broadway, with a hotel on one corner, a drugstore on another, the post office on the third and a movie house on the fourth. Within a block were three more theaters. The main ones were the Arcade and the Kozy, which advertised in the local newspapers several times a week, listing attractions which were changed every three days. There also were the Orpheum, for which ads appeared about once a week, and the Star, across the street from the Kozy on Broadway between 4th and 5th streets, which relied on its marquee to attract patrons. The Kozy ads always included the statement, "Prices always 10 cents and 25 cents." These were day and night prices.

During our earlier years, we attended the Arcade on Saturday mornings. It didn't matter what the main feature was, as we went to keep abreast of the cowboy serials, which always ended with a Tom Mix or Hoot Gibson cliff-hanger, so we had to go back to see what happened next.

We went to the Orpheum occasionally when it advertised a vaudeville, which usually featured a comedian and a line of dancing girls. Admission to shows was 25 cents. I remember a group which had a girl with a red heart tattooed on her thigh just below the skirt line. That was considered quite daring and her appearance insured a good crowd.

Some of the shows advertised at the Arcade were "Ruggles at Red Gap," with Lois Wilson and Edward Horton; "Why Men Leave Home," with Helen Chadwick and Lewis Stone; Jack London's "Call of the Wild," with Lois Wilson and Richard Dix; "Son of the

Sahara," with Claire Windsor and Bert Lytell; and "Shadows of Paris," with Pola Negri. Infrequently, the Arcade featured a vaudeville on weekends, in two acts with comedy, singing, dancing and acrobats. One 1923 show included Katherine McDonald in "Refugees."

At the Kozy, we could see "Souls in Bondage," with an "all-star cast," and an added feature; Charlie Chaplin in "Sunnyside," billed as his funniest; Gloria Swanson in "Prodigal Daughters;" "Wild Oranges," presented by King Vidor with Frank Mayo, Virginia Valli and Ford Sterling, with added short show; and Will Rogers in "The Comedy Sheik."

The Orpheum was the only true theater in Paducah. All the others were designed strictly for movies, with long rows of seats and aisles. All entrances were at the rear, except at the Arcade, which had its entrance with an arcade on Broadway. The arcade led to the movie room with seats at right angles to the entrance.

Orpheum seats were in a semi-circle with two tiers of box seats on each side. The degree of slant front to back was almost double that of the movie houses, the rows of seats were a little wider. There also were two balconies.

All movie houses had separate entrances for white and "colored," with the top balcony for the "colored." At first, the movies were silent and only in black & white.

This Was Downtown Paducah

The city still maintained the old Fowler wharf boat at the foot of Broadway, but it no longer handled commercial freight. It was used to house canoes and small craft and a number of riverboats still tied up alongside. West Kentucky Coal had a corrugated metal shack at the river side of the Petter steel warehouse at the foot of Kentucky Avenue. It was used by the black coal tenders to deliver coal to passing steamboats. The coal was loaded into "handies," which held several hundred pounds of coal. They had two handles on each end, so two men could walk the coal up the gangplank and dump it into the steamboat holds.

The old four-story Richmond House still occupied the northwest corner of 1st and Broadway. Although no longer in operation as a hotel, it was used as a transient home for drifters and indigent families passing through town. Hot meals and beds for the night were furnished, paid for by the city and a number of relief agencies.

On the river side of the southeast corner of 1st and Broadway was a warehouse for Armour & Company, with a railroad spur track in front and a truck loading dock facing the river and extending over the bank. Other buildings on the river side of 1st Street were the Petter steel warehouse with a track siding at Kentucky, and the Paducah Iron three-story building with a track spur on the river side facing the Paducah water pumping station and filtration plant. All of these buildings were torn down in 1940 to make way for the flood wall. Also removed at that time were the railroad spur tracks from the Illinois Central freight depot on Campbell Street along the river front to the Paducah Marine Ways.

Near the northeast corner of 7th Street and next door to my father's grocery was the Crystal Creamery ice cream plant. Just across the street, near the corner of 7th and Broadway was the Parisian Laundry & Cleaners. At that time, the Bradshaw & Weil Company was next to the Oehlschlaeger corner drugstore at 6th and Broadway and directly across the street from the Adolph Weil home, later to be the site of the Irvin Cobb Hotel. This fine old brick two-story home was surrounded by a waist-high iron picket fence. The Weils, who were elderly, could be seen taking daily walks on the sidewalk around their home. The Oehlschlaeger Drugstore was a popular place, with George at the prescription counter and sons, John and Frank, at the soda fountain.

Several taverns served the downtown trade, of which Heinie & Tyler was the most popular. It had a long "men only" bar and was a favorite luncheon place for downtown workers. There were more

more than a dozen barber and beauty shops downtown. We got our haircuts at the City Barber Shop, several doors down from the corner drugstore at 5th and Broadway, which was then Walker's and later Walgreen's. I followed my favorite barber when he moved to the Cobb shop. When he died, I went back to the City shop, now under the name of Conway's. All the old barbers are gone and the shop has only one chair. After 75 years, I have gone there for the longest time.

Western Union and Postal Telegraph maintained offices on lower Broadway and handled a lot of commercial traffic. The "dime" stores, Kresge and Woolworth, were in the middle of the Broadway block between 3rd and 4th streets. Kresge had a lunch counter that was very popular. The big stores downtown were Rudy's, Guthrie's and Rieke's, all within the same block on Broadway between 3rd and 4th streets. There were two shoeshine parlors near the corner of 4th and Broadway, across the street from one another. Each had about 12 chairs; shines were 10 cents.

Between Jefferson and Washington on 2nd and 3rd streets, were mostly wholesale and industrial firms. On lower Broadway, a few doors apart, were the Mitchell and Ellis machine shops, Jackson Foundry & Machine, Thompson's Blacksmith Shop next to Petter, Brown Brothers Boiler Shop on Broadway at Maiden Alley, several electrical shops, Hamilton's Mattress Factory, Cohen's Pawn Shop, and a number of fruit and vegetable shops and the Market House.

Some Downtown Places

We were in school in the '20s and '30s and went to neighborhood schools that were not yet integrated. There were no school buses, so we either walked, rode bicycle or later, had our parents take us. Most of the time, we walked. When in high school, I had an early morning paper route for the *News-Democrat* and rode my bike to school.

The schools I attended were: Robert E. Lee at 4th and Ohio, Thomas Jefferson at 8th and Madison, Washington Junior High at Broadway and 13th, and Augusta Tilghman High on Murrell Boulevard.

Other schools in town were: Longfellow at 12th and Jackson, Whittier at 1300 N. 12th, McKinley at Hayes and Bridge, Henry Clay at Guthrie Avenue and "B" Street, Arcadia Junior High at Clark and Lone Oak Road and Franklin at 1320 S. 6th St. There were two black schools: Dunbar at 25th and Yeiser and Garfield at 9th and Harris. The West Kentucky Vocational School and dormitory at 28th and Atkins became a reality in the 1920s and there was one private school, Dorian's at 4th and Washington.

Churches

There were a number of the downtown churches with large congregations. The Baptist church was at 5th and Jefferson, Kentucky Avenue Presbyterian was at 6th and Kentucky, First Christian was at 7th and Jeffferson, Evangelical and Reformed was at 427 S. 5th, Immanuel Baptist was at 408 Murrell Blvd. and Temple Israel was at 7th and Broadway. All have been torn down and new edifices built farther west. Churches still in use today include First Presbyterian at 7th and Jefferson, St. Francis deSales

Catholic at 6th and Broadway, Broadway United Methodist at 7th and Broadway and Grace Episcopal at 9th and Broadway.

Restaurants

Although there were a number of restaurants downtown, families did not eat out much. Some of the downtown restaurants that did a good business were Boswell's in the Palmer House, Rothrock's on Broadway, Mooney's across the street from the Market House and later on, the dining room of the Irvin Cobb Hotel.

Night Spots

In the early '20s, the Blue Bird Inn on S. Friendship Road featured dining and dancing. By the time I was out of school, it no longer existed. The main places for those of us in high school were the Peacock Garden, right next to the railroad overpass on Broadway, today the location of Dr. William Walden, DDS. When Buck Willingham graduated from Tilghman High School, he opened the Cat and the Fiddle night spot on the other side of the same overpass on the south side of Broadway. This later was renamed the Twinkling Star, a name that remained for decades. Another favorite spot was Albritton's Drugstore on the corner of 32nd and Broadway. All three places offered curb service featuring fountain drinks and sandwiches. After liquor became legal in 1933, there were two nightclubs a few miles out on the Cairo Road that became very popular for the younger crowd. They offered food, drinks and dancing to jukeboxes and an occasional live music.

Transportation

Rail service was active in the early days of Paducah. You could board the Illinois Central train at Union Station at 9 p.m., go to bed in your berth, sleep the night away and be in Louisville early the next morning. To go north or south by train, you could go to Fulton and catch the Panama Limited or the City of New Orleans, both express trains. Or you could take the Louisian, the slow one which made numerous stops along the way.

The Greyhound and Southern Limited bus lines ran frequently to all parts of the country. And if you wanted to go to Detroit, the Brooks Bus Line made several trips weekly each way, making pickups in Fulton, Mayfield, Murray, Paducah and other towns going north.

We did not have scheduled airline service, but did have two small airports: Howell Field on the Coleman Road and Iseman Field on the south side of town where Wal-mart is now situated. There were a number of local light aircraft owners.

An enormous amount of freight was handled by the Illinois Central freight house at 6th and Campbell and the NC&StL freight house at 3rd and Washington. People traveling east and west on Broadway and other parallel streets frequently had to wait at the crossings for long lines of freight cars to thread their way through town.

Although the steam paddle boats were gradually disappearing from the scene, there were a number of locally-owned companies providing freight movement by water. The West Kentucky Coal Company had several boats that hauled coal from their mines in Kentucky. The Igert fleet operated many small boats. Fred Olcott built boats and barges. The Marine Ways had several boats, including the A.I. Baker, named for Ann Baker, superintendent of the Ways. A good friend, James Curtis of Curtis & Mays and the Camera Shop, became a pilot on Standard Oil's Destrahan, West Kentucky Coal's Charles Richardson and the A.I. Baker.

Ferries and Bridges

To get to Metropolis, one had to drive to the Metropolis Lake Landing Road in West Paducah to catch the ferry. In May of 1929, the Paducah-Brookport Bridge was opened, cutting travel time to Illinois to mere minutes. When other bridges were constructed there were toll charges for years, until the state took them over.

Streets and Roads

Most Paducah side streets were gravel. Broadway was paved with curb and gutter only west to 26th Street. It then narrowed to two lanes of asphalt going west and then south to Lone Oak. There was a large hollow on Kentucky Avenue between 12th and 17th streets. The south side was filled in with about 45,000 carloads of dirt for the Illinois Central Railroad shops built there in 1927. The north side was later filled in for new home construction.

Downtown Businesses

Among the downtown businesses in the 1920s and '30s were the Paducah Marine Ways, the city's oldest industry, at 1st and Washington Street, the Sangravl Company on the Tennessee River, Federal Materials Company on North 2nd Street between Jefferson and Madison, the International Shoe Company at 2nd and Jefferson, Langstaff-Orm Lumber Company on 2nd Street between Clark and Tennessee, the Paducah Lumber Company at 900 N. 9th and the firms of Worthy Manufacturing, which became M. Fine Company shirt factory at 1117 N. 8th, which were in operation for a span of about 10 years. When the factory was built during the Depression, employees of that company and other Paducah firms were paid half of their wages in script and half in dollars.

There were a number of downtown hotels, including the Irvin Cobb at 6th and Broadway, the Palmer House at 5th and Broadway, the Oxford at 5th and Jefferson, the Sinnott at 2nd and Broadway and the Economy Hotel on Broadway between 1st and 2nd streets.

Since many businesses and residents used coal for heating, there were a number of coal dealers. The most prominent were West Kentucky Coal, St. Bernard Coal, Bradley Brothers, King Coal and Faughn Coal. It was rumored that another company called "Midnight Coal" was in operation along the railroad tracks. It was said to operate only at night when "pickers" would mount the open gondolas of freight trains as they crawled slowly along the rail near the south yards and toss off large hunks of coal. By daylight, all coal scattered along the tracks would be "sold."

There were still a few companies in Paducah using horses and wagons for deliveries, such as milk and ice, which were delivered door to door. The horses that pulled these wagons got so used to their regular routes that they moved along without a word from their drivers. The Thompson Transfer Company, on Broadway between 10th and 11th streets, had several big teams which made pickups and deliveries from both freight depots to local businesses. There were many "express" men who offered hauling service all over town. Most parked their teams on the curb on Kentucky Avenue between 2nd and 3rd, awaiting calls at a telephone box nearby. There were several livery stables and blacksmith shops downtown that shoed horses, but these would close as automobiles replaced horse-drawn wagons.

Automobiles and dealers

Most automobile dealers had their display rooms and warehouses downtown. None of the old dealerships of the '20s are still around. The old model cars bore names most people today have never heard. Gus Edwards Motor Sales at 311-312 Kentucky Ave. sold the Columbia Six. Choate-Melton Hudson at 504 Broadway were dealers for Essex, Hudson and Cadillac. C.N. Baker Motor Company sold Hupmobile and Miller Motors at 620 Broadway sold Durant and Star cars. There was also a car named Moon, with a few sold here, probably made by the same company that made the Star.

A few early car names are still with us today. Ford, the most popular car of the 1920s, was sold by the Foreman Automobile

Company at 121-127 N. 4th St. Paul Follis of Follis & Son was the dealer for Chrysler. Payne-Burnett Company at 611 Broadway, owned by Dewey Payne and Bill Burnett were Studebaker, Erskin and DeSoto dealers. Their most loyal customer was the 606 Taxi Company (telephone number 606), which used Studebakers exclusively and was located in the Payne-Burnett building. Dubois-Ashcraft Motor Sales was at 415 Kentucky Ave. and was a Dodge and Plymouth dealer. Abell Motors on North 4th Street handled Chevrolet and C.N. Baker on Kentucky near 7th Street was an Oldsmobile dealer. Broadway Motors sold Lincoln and Ford and Dixie Motors had Chryslers. Warren Motors was a Buick dealership. Katterjohn-Melton handled Hudson and Essex and Overstreet Motors sold Oakland and Pontiac. All the auto companies were situated from 9th Street east toward downtown.

An ad in the July 23, 1924 issue of the *Paducah Evening Sun* by Miller Motors listed the price of a Durant touring model, a four-door cloth top car, at $976 and a sport touring model at $1,265. A sport sedan cost $1,700 and had balloon tires and four-wheel brakes. The Star touring model was shown at $605 and a sport sedan was $1,065. Studebakers cost $675 for a touring model. A light-six was $1,550 and big-six sedan was $2,750. Black was the only color choice.

Almost all dealers had space for no more than three cars in their showrooms and space for backup stocks of from six to a dozen in other parts of their buildings. I do not remember seeing outside new car lots, though dealers displayed used cars on outside lots. They were usually adjacent to the new car showrooms. Service and repair stations were in the backs of the buildings.

Paducah Gas Plant

Memory Lane

Paducah Life in the 1920s

ife in Paducah in the 1920s was pretty spartan by today's standards. There were no automobile bridges over the rivers, so one had to take a ferry to get to Illinois. There were no four-lane highways and many of the good roads were gravel.

We didn't have natural gas then, but used coal-tar gas, manufactured at Paducah's plant at 2nd and Monroe. The gas was dirty and produced only 500 Btu per cubic foot, compared to today's cleaner natural gas at 1000 btu. Most families cooked with kerosene, commonly called coal oil. Heating and cooking with electricity was too expensive. Electricity was available only in the city. It became available in the rural areas in 1935, when the Rural Electrification Administration (REA) came into being.

There was no air conditioning or automatic refrigeration. Food and drinks were kept cool in iceboxes. Several ice manufacturing plants in Paducah made daily door-to-door home deliveries. One put a card in the window to indicate the amount of ice wanted each day. Most people had milk delivered to their back doors or placed in metal containers furnished by the ice companies. There were about five milk companies with delivery routes to homes and grocers. City Consumers, Dudley and Dexter were the big ones.

We had no local radio stations and few radios. The nearest radio station was in Hopkinsville. Television would not be invented for about three decades.

Our first telephone number was 584. To make a long distance call, something we rarely did, one asked the operator to make the call for them. It sometimes took as long as 30 minutes to get a call through. Businesses used Western Union and Postal Telegraph to send and receive messages. Receiving a telegram at home usually meant a serious illness or a death in the family.

Airmail did not come into being until 1926. We had no commercial airline service and only a few privately-owned planes. They flew from Iseman Field on the Clark's River Road. It was owned by Charles Iseman of the Iseman Lumber Company.

One summer during my high school days, a number of us were asked to park cars at the airfield Saturday and Sunday afternoons when Iseman offered 30-minute rides over town in a Ford tri-motored plane for $2. The field was crowded both days and flights continued until dark. On Sunday, we who had been parking cars all afternoon were called just before dark to take the very last flight. This was to be our pay for the two days of work. I don't know how the others felt, but I was thrilled to have my first ride in a big plane. It was payment enough.

Life was pretty serene then. Our wants and needs were fewer, crime was minimal, streets were safe, family ties were stronger, morals were higher and most people attended church regularly. Entertainment was usually local. Traffic was less hectic and life proceeded at a more leisurely pace. No one would want to return to the conditions of those days. Yet, in a lot of ways, those were the good old days.

Strolling Down Memory Lane

Take a mental stroll with me through the downtown Paducah business district as it was in 1923, when my family moved here from Memphis, Tennessee. At that time, I was nine years old and didn't know where anything was located. But over the years, going to school, working in the downtown ever since, I have come to know Paducah well. I can still remember most of the names and places of those earlier years.

Our first home was upstairs in the Napoleon Apartments, a two-story four-unit brick building near the southwest corner of 5th and Washington. It faced the twin-building Kennett Apartments just across the street, owned by the Gardners, an old-time Paducah family who also owned a furniture store on Broadway. The surrounding area was primarily residential, but was only two blocks from the downtown Broadway business district. Now, very few residences are located there, with the city hall and Dolly McNutt Plaza occupying most of the area.

It was only a four-block walk to Dad's first grocery at 621 Broadway, in a building constructed by the Saunders Fowler family, and now occupied by Bradshaw & Weil Insurance Company At that time, the grocery was next door to the Crystal Creamery Company, makers of ice cream. On the east side was the Payne-Burnett Studebaker Company, with its used car lot in between. The 606 Taxi had its office in the Payne-Burnett building and its Studebaker taxis in their garage.

Across the street, on the southeast corner of 7th and Broadway in the Scott Building was the Parisian Laundry & Cleaners. Today, the Camera Shop and Curtis-Mays Studio own that property.

Leaving Dad's store and walking on the north side toward the river, we would pass the Dan McFadden Portrait Studio and the offices of Steinfield & Steinfield, Optometrists. On the corner was Oehlschlaeger's Drugstore, operated by George and his two sons, John, a pharmacist, and Frank, who was at the soda fountain. Directly across the street on the southwest corner, was the beautiful home of the Adolph Weils, soon to be torn down for the Irvin Cobb Hotel.

We next cross 6th Street and notice a 20-foot-tall totem pole mounted in the grass on the corner lot. Behind it, set back about 15 feet from the sidewalk was an old red brick one-story former residence that was converted into an office building. It contained offices for Roy Manchester, the Boy Scout executive. The Rotary Club office was located there as well, as Manchester was club secretary. Also there were the McCracken County American Red Cross and the McCracken County Public Health League.

Sixth to Fifth Street

Kreutzer Candy Store was beside the Boy Scout building and had a large metal awning which hung out over the sidewalk. Then came Van Aart Florist, Sam Dalbey's Electric Store and the Guthrie Building, previously known as the Fraternity Building. On the corner was the old stone three-story post office and federal building with the statue of Chief Paduke and water fountain by the front steps. On the south side of Broadway from 6th to 5th, was St. Francis deSales Catholic Church, next to the Sloan office building and apartments, Rothrock's Restaurant, the Leroy Music Store, Columbia office building (where the Columbia Theater is now), Arcade Hatters, Choate-Melton Hudson Auto Agency, the Arcade Theater, Lloyd Emory's Arcade Fountain and the Sinnott Smoke Shop on the corner.

Fifth to Fourth Street

Continuing east, we cross 5th Street where the Palmer House Hotel dominates the intersection. This four-story hotel was built in 1892 and was Paducah's first skyscraper, with passenger elevators and steam heat. Gilbert-Bennett's Drugstore anchored the corner at street level. Two of my school mates, Jeff "Sweets" Robinson and Paul Martin, jerked sodas at the fountain and had quite a following among teenage customers. There were five downtown Broadway corner drugstores, all with soda fountains.

The Palmer House Chocolate Shop was the first store as you came out of the Broadway entrance to the hotel. Then there were Wanner's Jewelers, George Rock Shoes, the Kozy Theater, Harris Brothers Men's Store, Weille's Department Store, Bright's Ladies' Shop, Clay Kidd Stationers and another Gilbert-Bennett Drugstore on the corner.

On the south side of Broadway from 5th to 4th, were

Walker's Drugstore on the corner, Oakley's Cafe, Schmaus Florist, the Star Theater, Henneberger's Hardware, Railway Express, Gleave's Furniture, List Drugstore in the middle of the block, E.P. Gilson Paint, the Dixie Cafe, Paducah Electric Power Company, Preno's Billiards, Superior Merchant Tailors and on the corner, the Winter Hotel with the Newark Shoe Store on the main floor.

Fourth to Third Street

On the northeast corner of 4th was Paducah's tallest structure, the City National Bank building, built in 1911. On its top nine floors were the offices of most of the doctors and dentists in town. Rudy's Department Store was next door in an ell-shaped building with entrances on Broadway and 4th Street. Next door to it was Wolff Jewelers, then Lowenthal's Ladies' Wear, Woolworth's, McLaughlin Music Store, Segenfelter's Drugs, Cochran's Shoes and Nagel & Meyers Jewelers.

On the south side of Broadway at 4th, Rieke's Dry Goods was on the corner and next door was Guthrie's Department Store. Next was Kresge's dime store, Paducah Candy Kitchen, Victor's Ladies' Clothing, Zula Cobb's Millinery Store, Henry Diehl Men's Shoes, Edelen's Ladies' Store, D.E. Wilson Book Store and soda fountain, Chris Haralambo's Confections and the First National Bank on the corner.

Third to Second Street

Let's walk the next block on the south side of Broadway from 3rd to 2nd streets. On the corner was the Citizen's Bank. There were several residential apartments on the second floor with the entrance on 3rd Street. Parrish Jewelers was next door. Next was the Cigar Store, which was a front for one of the several "horse parlors" downtown. Behind the small cigar counter was a door leading into the large room with a "tote board" all along one wall where an attendant with headphones on a raised platform would record racing results as they occurred. There was always a group of men sitting in chairs watching the board. An attendant out front knew the clientele and admitted only people they knew or who were cleared by the owners. The police were aware of the "action," but tolerated the business, except on rare occasions when there was a crackdown.

Next door was the Singer Sewing Machine Company, Ehreafeld-Ritter and Harry Herwitz ladies' stores, Hank & Davis Paint, Hank Brothers Hardware, Western Union Telegraph, Randall & Osheroff Tailor Shop, the Boston Shoe Shop and I. Cohen Men's Store and Pawn Shop on the corner.

Across the street at the northeast corner of 3rd Street and Broadway, was Wallerstein's Men's Store. Next to it was the Ohio Valley building containing the Ohio Valley Bank & Trust Company, Ohio Valley Fire & Marine Company, Gardner Real Estate and W.M. Husband's law offices. The Mechanic's Trust & Savings Bank and Bradshaw & Weil Insurance were in the next building. Then followed M. Manas Jewelers, M. Marks Men's Clothing, Lang Brothers Drugs, Warren's Jewelers, Cartwrignt Billiards, Whitehead's Cafe, Hayes Barber Shop, Rosenfield's Men's Store, Michael Brothers Saddlery & Hardware and on the corner, the Sinnott Hotel.

We are now at 2nd and Broadway. Just across the street on the south side of Broadway is the Market House. Imagine you are seeing it in the '20s. It is divided into three sections. In the front section are farmers and growers selling flowers and plants. As you go through the first set of swinging doors you see the stall of the Dumaine brothers, selling fancy fruit. Then a number of butcher stalls line each side of the room. Among the owners' names on the wall are Riley Jones, T.A. Jones, Metzger, Rector, Kolb, Petter and Herzog. We then go through a second set of doors into the third section where all the produce growers have stalls. The list includes the Rottgerings, William, Lewis and Henry; the Legeays; the Schmidts; the Bichons; the Steinhauers; the Yopps and the McCutchens. There are a total of 66 stalls.

On the south side of Broadway between 2nd and 1st going toward the river, we pass Frank Men's Store, Smith Shoe Repair Shop, Tagnon's Tailor Shop, Campbell's Sporting Goods, Mason's Welding Shop, Jewel Auto Supply Company, F.H. Nieman's Luggage

Shop, Sherrer's Piano Repair Shop and Ohio Valley Canvas Company. Across Maiden Alley is the Fowler-Wolff Sheet Metal Works, Tom Roger's Paducah Printing Company, Jacob Bamberger's Furniture, Ellis Brothers Machine Shop, Kilcoyne Electric Shop and on the corner, Brown's Welding and Sheet Metal.

All the buildings on the south side from Maiden Alley to the corner of 1st Street were later acquired by the Petter Supply Company. On the north side from 2nd to 1st street were American Confectionery, Sparks Barber Shop, Charles Leake Printers, the Economy Hotel, Mitchell's Machine and Electric Shop, the Brown Hotel, Illinois Hotel, Joe Klein's Cigars, Morton's Barber Shop, J.W. Dunn's Fruits, David Bullmer's Wholesale Meats and on the corner, the Southern Hotel.

At the foot of Broadway was the Paducah Wharf Boat Company, offices of the St. Louis & Tennessee River Packet Company, Paducah & Metropolis Packet Company, Nashville Navigation Company, Dycusburg & Paducah Daily Packet Company and the J.C. Lunchroom. On the southeast corner was Armour & Company.

How Things Have Changed

*M*any changes have taken place since our family moved here over seven decades ago. Many old firms which were active and vital parts of the community no longer exist. Many beautiful old landmarks have been demolished. The owners of most of the downtown stores and businesses are no longer living. The companies that provided our biggest payrolls and employment are but memories.

Among those I remember are Claussner Hosiery Mills at 2nd and Tennessee and 28th and Clark; Priester Hosiery Mills at 9th and

Kentucky, Southern Textile Machinery at 3rd and Norton, International Shoe at 2nd and Jefferson, McKee Button Company at 3rd and Elizabeth, Modine at 29th and Jackson, Magnavox on North 8th, the Illinois Central Railroad shops on Kentucky Avenue and Cohankus Manufacturing Company on North 8th. All are gone. Also gone are many service companies like Paducah Ice Manufacturing and City Consumers for our milk and dairy products; wholesale distributors such as Barger & Golightly, Peck Brothers, Dumaine Brothers and H&H Produce Company, which supplied us with fresh fruits and vegetables. Covington Brothers, Clark-Lack and M. Livingston supplied local grocers with their staple goods. All these local companies have been replaced by the giant chain supermarkets.

Wallace Park, which covered a 75-acre tract between Buckner Lane and Blandville Road, was the largest park in town and the most popular. It was accessible by a streetcar line that ran by and was terminated on Forest Circle. With its grandstand, baseball diamond, golf course, lake and shaded picnic areas, it was in full use during the summer season. When Paducah competed with eight other west Kentucky cities for the state normal school in the early '20s, Wallace Park was offered for the school campus. The Depression of the 1930s saw the end of the park and the beginning of efforts to secure other acreage, which became Noble Park.

Around the '40s and '50s, the face of Paducah began to change drastically. Many downtown merchants who either lived in lower town or over their businesses began to move out to the western part of town.

Around the '50s, many old landmarks were razed. The old city hall and number one fire station were replaced with new structures. The Masonic Hall at 5th and Kentucky, which had served originally as a college, then a high school and in later years housed many civic and trade organizations, was demolished. Paducah's first YMCA, which was next to the old post office in the late 1890s, was moved to the northeast corner of 6th and Broadway, then found its last home at 7th and Broadway, just west of the Broadway United Methodist Church. Paducah Junior college then bought it and used it until the new Paducah Community College was built on the Blandville Road. The church acquired the site, demolished the building and built Igert hall.

The beautiful Carnegie Library at 9th and Broadway, which was given to the city in 1903, suffered a fire in 1963, which caused extensive damage and necessitated demolition. It was replaced by the new public library across from Dolly McNutt Plaza.

All the downtown movies are gone, having fled to the mall. Although the Arcade and Columbia buildings are still standing, they are idle. It is hoped they will be preserved, remodeled and put to productive use.

The many boarding houses that were all over town, including some downtown, are gone and replaced by new hotels, motels, fast food stores and bed and breakfasts. Those I remember include the Carlson Boarding House at 15th and Broadway, which catered to the Illinois Central shop workers a block away. Many friends of mine who were shop employees ate lunch there. In the summers before being called to the Army, I ate there many times. I also remember the Martin House near 9th and Madison, where a good meal cost 35 cents. It later became famous as the Ninth Street House.

Strawberry Queens

Strawberry harvest time meant parades and a touch of royalty. In the late 1930s and early 1940s, Paducah was host for the annual West Kentucky Strawberry Festival held during the May-June harvest. Activities included boat rides, parades, band music, street dancing, coronation ceremonies, the queen's ball, berry judging and voting for candidates for the coveted title of Western Kentucky Strawberry Queen. A candidate was required to be the daughter of a grower.

The first festival was held in 1937 and the first queen was Bennie Owen Allen, teenage daughter of T.O. Allen of Kevil. Her six maids of honor were Mary Ellen Bradshaw, Martha Sue Mays, Caroline Tanner, Dixie Myers, Sue Judd and May E. Felts, all of Kevil. Queen Bennie is now Mrs. Fred Crice and lives on Audubon

1937 Strawberry Queen, Mary Ellen Bradshaw

Drive.

Other queens and festivals included:

- in 1938 - the queen was Mary Ellen Bradshaw. Since 1938 was the silver anniversary of the McCracken County Growers Association, the event promised to be the biggest yet. It featured the arrival of the queen and her court at the foot of Broadway in a boat, where they were saluted by trumpeter John Wright Polk and greeted by Mayor Edgar Washburn, City Manager L.V. Bean and other city and county officials.

- in 1939 - Frances King won the crown. She and her court arrived on the cruiser, Domino, at Barkley Park, where the coronation ceremony took place, were escorted in open cars to the Irvin Cobb for refreshments and then led a parade to the Ritz, their host for the two days.

Queen Bradshaw receiving keys to Paducah, 1937

-in 1940 - the Strawberry Queen was Sally Stahl. In addition to all the local festivities, she received an all-expense 15-day trip to Hollywood and San Francisco. At the beginning of World War II, she moved to Detroit and became "Rosie the Riveter," working on airplanes for the war effort.

- in 1941 - there was a separate queen for each of the 17 participating counties - 13 from Kentucky, three from Illinois and one from Tennessee.

- in 1948 - McCracken County representative for queen was Aimee Warner, who later became Mrs. Bobby Grimm.

Boarding and Rooming Houses

There were five boarding houses I remember from my younger days. The A.H. Cobb family had one at 712 Kentucky Ave., a few doors across the street from us. On some Sundays, our family ate at Skip Elliott's boarding house at 6th and Monroe. When my Uncle Grady moved to Paducah to work for Dad's grocery, he got room and board at the C.M. Nelson house at 822 Jefferson St.

In the mid-'30s when Mrs. Annie Laurie Dunn came to work at Petter's as Stanley Petter's secretary, she and her husband, W.L., a machinist who had moved from Vicksburg to work for the ICRR, lived at Mrs. Nellie Martin's boarding house at 323 Ninth St. That house has a lot of history, as it was built by George Wallace for his wife, May, the daughter of Benjamin Wisdom, one of Paducah's early millionaires, and a sister of Nellie, wife of the Rev. William Ed Cave, pastor of the First Presbyterian Church. Later, it became the Ninth Street House, a popular restaurant, owned by the Curtis Grace family.

Carlson's boarding house at 1500 Broadway was a very popular noon eating place for many ICRR shop men. It was only a block from the shops and they could come over in their work clothes and get a big meal and be back within the 45-minute lunch period. At that time, South 15th Street was open from Broadway to Kentucky. When the Sears store moved from downtown it occupied the whole block from 15th to 16th, including the Carlson property.

Mrs. Carlson served at a large table always loaded down with bowls of vegetables and three kinds of meat. She always had fried chicken and several times a week she had calves liver. During the summer months when my mother stayed with my two sisters who lived in Chicago, I'd go to the Carlson's for lunch several times a week. It was a very sumptuous meal which cost 35 cents, dessert included.

Youth Activities

and

Special People

Boy Scouts of America

*J*oining the Boy Scouts was one of the best things I ever did. Quite soon after moving here, I became aware of the organization. The Scout office was in a little old one-story brick building set back on the northeast corner of 6th and Broadway, directly across from St. Francis deSales Church. There was a totem pole close to the front walk.

One had to be 12 to join, so on the day I reached that age, I walked into the office and joined. My parents took me to Wallerstein's Men's Store, the official Scout outfitters, and bought me a complete outfit, including a Smokey Bear hat, Sam Browne belt, khaki shirt and pants, brown shoes and socks. When we got home, they took my picture in my new uniform in the front yard of our home at 715 Kentucky Avenue.

Roy C. Manchester was executive in charge of all the many Scout troops in Paducah and the surrounding area. His secretaries over the 15 years I was in Scouting included Miss Merle Warner (later Mrs. George Katterjohn), Miss Christine Allison and Miss Dorothy Weiman, who was a member of my high school class.

Almost all downtown churches had Scout troops. I joined Troop 5 at the Presbyterian Church on the northeast corner of 7th and Jefferson. Over the years I was active, my Scoutmasters were Gus and Tuttle Lockwood, Gus Hank Sr., and Nat Dortch. Other leaders at camp were Russell Mills, Frank Rinkleff, Sam Traughber, Raymond Snodgrass and Wayman Parsons. Also long-time policeman and veteran camp regular John "Daddy" Hessian. We met once a week at the church, were taught all about Scouting, its mottoes, creeds and rules. Afterwards, we engaged in some form of exercise or games. Dodgeball was one of our favorite games.

I stayed in Scouts for over 15 years, worked diligently to earn the 21 merit badges to qualify for the Eagle Scout badge and had the distinction of being Paducah's 50th Eagle Scout on my 14th birthday. I served as Scoutmaster at McKinley School on the south side of town for several years and became assistant Scoutmaster to Tony

Barron White, Eagle Scout, age 13, 1927

*Barron White,
Home from
Pakentuck Scout Camp*

Johnson, the manual training teacher at Arcadia School, who started Paducah's first, and I believe only, Sea Scout troop.

One winter, we built a sailboat during Monday night meetings at the school and sailed it on the Ohio River the next summer.
It was a nice efficient little boat with a mainsail, jib and centerboard.
All the strakes were put together with copper rivets on 12-inch cen-
ters. We learned to tack against the wind, put about and to maneu-
ver in every direction. The river current had to be considered and it
seemed we were always downstream when the wind died down in
the late afternoon. Kentucky Lake did not exist at that time.

My brother Harry, two years younger than I, joined Scouts
and we attended Scout camps at Dixon Springs, Ill., and Pakentuck,

near Ozark, Ill. We were together with boys and men from all walks of life. Many became lifelong friends, including Sam Livingston; Jimmy Rieke; Bill Lockwood; Tuttle Lockwood; Bill and Ed "Hawk" Cave; Burgess, Ed and Joe Scott; Luke Nichol; Mahlon Shelbourne; Ralph Nagel; Ed Robertson; Bill Ezzell; Jimmie Huston; Murray Rogers; Frank Davis; Louis Grimmer; Harry J. Livingston; John Polk; Richard Ragland; Clark Craig; Bill Fisher; and Herman Graham.

Totem Pole

Boy Scout Totem Pole

ew Paducahans remember the totem pole that stood in front of the Boy Scout headquarters on the northeast corner of 6th and Broadway. The pole was carved by Dan Galvin, a retired molder and pattern maker who was fascinated with Boy Scout activities. He conceived the idea of a downtown sign to mark the location of the Boy Scout headquarters in Paducah, which was the home of Indian Chief Paduke.

Galvin procured a cedar telephone pole 20 feet in height and nine inches in diameter, and using only a hammer and chisel, carved Indian figures and signs on the pole. Chief Paduke's face was carved twice near the top.

On the back and sides, Galvin painted the names of Paducahans who were active in the Boy Scout movement, including Scout Executive Roy Manchester, Freddie Roth, policeman John "Daddy" Hessian, Dr. P.H. Stewart, Tuttle

Lockwood, George Langstaff Jr., J.T. Donovan, Martin Yopp, Alfred Levy, Ed G. Scott, W.P. Paxton, Richard Rudy, Frank Weiland and James Wheeler. A few years after the totem pole was erected, Scoutmaster Tony Johnson, a manual training instructor, added an eagle with outstretched wings to the top.

The pole was taken down when the old Alumni Building, which housed Boy Scout headquarters, was demolished to make room for a new A&P grocery building. It was moved one block north behind the Knights of Columbus building on the corner of 6th and Jefferson.

Now, more than 70 years later, that pole still stands in the backyard of Galvin's grandson, Tommie Galvin, after having been relocated several times. Although it went through the 1937 flood, it still looks pretty good, although some of the names are faint. Tom says it is gradually being destroyed by woodpeckers and may not remain standing for too many years more.

Newspaper Carrier Boy

In 1927, some of my friends were getting jobs carrying newspapers. I wanted a bicycle, so I applied for a job at the *Paducah News-Democrat* office on North 4th Street. This was a morning paper owned by George Goodman. I was hired and assigned to a route in the west end beyond the city limits, starting at Albritton's Drugstore at 32nd and Broadway and including most of the Avondale area, out to the intersection of Buckner Lane and Pines Road.

All carriers reported around 3 a.m. to Ed McMahon, who distributed papers to them. At one of the benches in the back of the building, we rolled our papers and placed them in cloth sacks which were slung onto our bicycles between the handle bars and seats.

Those with large routes had sacks so full their knees were spread so wide it was hard to get their feet on the whole pedals. We would then head out and deliver all our papers with a daily handful of "starts" and "stops" to enable us to deliver to the current list of customers. We were required to "porch" all papers and to do so would ride by the house and throw the paper from the sidewalk, hoping it would land on the porch. If we missed, we had to get off the bike and retrieve the paper from the sidewalk and throw it onto the porch. Many of the homes on my first route were set back in the yards, making it difficult to accurately throw from the sidewalk or street.

We had to finish our routes before 6 a.m. and report to the office by phone. If a customer reported we had missed their house, we were docked 25 cents for each miss. Since the route paid only $1.75 a week, we could not afford many misses.

In those days, there were not many homes on my route. Buckner Lane was gravel and beyond 38th Street was mainly farmland. Exall's Pit was at Buckner Lane and Pines Road and was a swimming hole most of us frequented occasionally. Exall's apple orchard covered much of the acreage on the south side of Buckner Lane from 45th Street to the Pines Road intersection. Jack Cole had a cider mill on the north side of Buckner at 45th, formerly the site where Citizen's Bank President Fred Nagel built his home, now the residence of Mr. and Mrs. Daniel Keys. Beyond the cider mill was a large wooded area. The area around the intersection of Pines Road and Friedman Lane contained summer homes of some of Paducah's businessmen. Most of the houses were at the backs of the lots and had fences and gates guarding the entrances. For those subscribers, we had to dismount and walk the papers to the houses.

After two years, I was assigned a mid-town route, which was easier, as it was closer, shorter and within a four-block-square area with sidewalks. I started deliveries at 12th and Kentucky, made a delivery in the Illinois Central Railroad roundhouse, then went west on Kentucky at 17th Street, over to Monroe and back to 12th, making deliveries on all the streets in between. I carried papers into the Illinois Central Hospital to patients on both floors. I parked my bike at the back entrance and walked up one floor and down the other. Since most patients were there only a short time, some just a few days, as they were admitted and released, I got change orders almost daily. The route paid $2 a week.

Out of my earnings, I paid for my bike. I bought several from the Reynolds Cycle Shop on South 3rd Street, next door behind the First National Bank, later the People's Bank. Reynolds had a payment plan of 25 cents a week, so he was able to sell to most of the paper carriers I knew.

One morning when returning from my route in the west end, I was run over by a postman on his way to work.. It was a dark, overcast day, just before dawn, with a slight mist in the air. He had turned out of South 31st Street toward town and I was pedaling under the railroad overpass going in the same direction when he struck me. Fortunately, I fell underneath and between the wheels of his Model T Ford and although bruised and scratched, suffered no injuries or ill effects and was able to get up and ride to town with him. My bicycle was crushed and beyond repair. His insurance company paid for a new bike.

When I started carrying papers, we lived near the corner of 7th and Kentucky Avenue. I continued to carry papers until my senior year at Tilghman High School, when we lived on Harahan Boulevard. I knew many of the boys who were carriers during those years. Some became friends at Scout camp and at school. Riding a bicycle for four years was good for building leg muscles and enhanced my ability to make the track team in school.

Paducah, A Baseball Town

Paducah has always been a baseball town, interested in teams from the major leagues on down. Kitty League players had many first class games at the old Wallace Park. In the spring of 1927, B.B. Hook, who owned and operated Hook's

Drugstore at the corner of 3rd and Kentucky, opened Hook's Park out on North 8th Street on ground opposite the old Magnavox plant, now Hannan Supply. Paducah held membership intermittently in the Kitty League and many minor league games were played there.

Every year there was a great deal of interest in the World Series. In the early and mid-1920s, very few people could receive radio broadcasts of the games. No network programs carried them, so the games could be heard only on a few stations in larger cities. Many people had to rely on the daily newspapers to get the results. In the mid-1920s both Paducah newspapers, the *Paducah Evening Sun* on South 3rd Street and the *Paducah News-Democrat* on North 4th, operated baseball boards to display game action. The "Sun" board, called "the Playograph," was mounted at the second floor level of the newspaper office.

A baseball diamond was painted on the face with players represented by moveable squares. As games were in progress, players would be moved around the board to simulate the action as the newspapers received it by radio. The ball would be pitched to the plate and moved around the board to mimic play. Runs, hits and errors were illustrated at the side. Newspaper staff members hidden behind the board would activate the play.

The "Sun" used Dick Meachem, Joe Phillips, George Burnett and Henry Weil. Every day hundreds of people crowded the streets, which were roped off from traffic, to watch the board and listen to those working the board announce the action by megaphone. Now obsolete, this was in use for many years.

Young Men's Christian Association

here has not been a Young Men's Christian Association (YMCA) in Paducah since 1934. The YMCA, however, was alive and well here, on and off, for about 75 years prior. The first record of the organization was in 1859 when the *Paducah Herald*, a newspaper published by John C. Noble, reported that the YMCA met at Ratcliffe's Hall, at Market (2nd Street) and Broadway. Listed as president was M.H. Fisk, principal of Paducah High School. Vice presidents were A.R. Lang, tobacco dealer; L.M. Gardner, attorney; W.L. Fuqua, constable; Edward Woolfolk, produce merchant; and J.H. Roe, attorney. C.H. Hess was secretary and George Cochran was treasurer and corresponding secretary. (John C. Noble was the father of Bob Noble after whom Noble Park is named.) According to YMCA archives in St. Paul, Minn., the Paducah YMCA went defunct after several years and was re-established in 1895.

A picture of a two-story white building with the words, "Young Men's Christian Association" painted on it was printed in a 1900 souvenir edition of a Paducah newspaper. The building had a low picket fence across its front at the sidewalk, which extended across the wide open lot on the right side. The 1956 historical picture booklet, "100 Years of Progress," shows a picture of the old white stone post office built in 1885 which shows the same building with the YMCA sign on the left side with the open lot and picket fence.

An 1893 architect's drawing shows a building at 531 Broadway identified as the YMCA. This is the northeast corner of 6th and Broadway, directly across from St. Francis deSales Catholic Church. The drawing indicates an ell-shaped building extending along 6th Street to more than halfway down the block. YMCA archives show there were 100 active members in Paducah in 1896 when George Langstaff was president. In 1900 the membership had increased to 140 and R.E. Ashbrook was president.

Records show the YMCA was still at 6th and Broadway in 1904, but that in 1908, there was no YMCA and the corner lot was occupied by the Paducah Commercial Club. There are no records of a YMCA from 1904 to 1922, when the association was listed as occupying rooms 203 and 204 in the City National Bank building on the corner of 4th and Broadway. H.L. Meyers was president; William Vogel, secretary.

In 1926, the YMCA moved to 707-719 Broadway, the former residence of Dr. David G. Murrell, the physician in charge of the Illinois Central Hospital on Broadway. The home had under-

YMCA, Paducah Junior College, 707 Broadway

gone extensive remodeling, adding a large two-story brick building with a large swimming pool on the first floor and gymnasium on the second floor over the pool, beside and behind the former residence.

When we moved to Paducah in 1923, the house at 707 Broadway was occupied by the J.E. Bugg family. Their son Bill, who was several years older than I, became a good friend. For years he worked for Nat Dortch at Dortch's tobacco plant on Kentucky Avenue. Bill married Rebecca "Becky" Boyd.

The YMCA was going strong during my high school years, 1927-1931. I spent a lot of time in the swimming pool, passed my life-saving test and became a member of the Paducah Swim Team, which practiced there weekly during the winter months. Our Red Cross life-saving instructor and swim coach was Paul Twitchell, who later gained fame as the founder and leader of his own religion, Eckankar. Members of our swim team included Euclid Covington, George Barkley, Ed Scott, Burgess Scott, Joe Scott, Luke Nichol, Gus Smith and Albert Otto. After Paducah Junior College acquired the building, we continued to use the pool for several years.

John N. "Daddy" Hessian

I left Jefferson Grade School in 1927 to enter seventh grade at Washington Junior High, which was on Broadway between 12th and 13th streets. A number of my male classmates and I were selected to be members of the school patrol, whose job was to help students cross the street during the noon lunch period. We wore white Sam Browne belts to identify us while on duty. Our leader was John Hessian, a long-time member of the Paducah Police Department, who was assigned to traffic duty in his latter years. Hessian loved children and his little friends affectionately called him "Daddy." He watched vigilantly over all the hundreds of children at lunch time and when classes were dismissed in the morning and afternoon.

Hessian was credited with preventing many accidents on Broadway, a main thoroughfare to and from downtown. He took a personal interest in all the children and was always glad to have a group of them clustered around him. He was appointed playground officer by the school.

Boy Scout Executive Roy Manchester took an interest in Hessian and for a number of years took him to the annual Scout summer camp at Pakentuck, Ill. He was there during my four years at camp. He lived in the headquarters building with the officials and was around the Scouts for all of their activities. He was surrogate father, chaplain and parent for all Scouts, particularly the younger ones who were on their first trip and lonesome and homesick. He was beloved by all whose lives he touched.

Daddy Hessian retired in 1934 after serving 40 years on the police force. He died two years later.

Ma and Hop Little

Our family operated three grocery stores in downtown Paducah in the 1920s and 1930s. One store was located on the northeast corner of 5th and Jefferson and I worked there off and on some Saturdays and during the summer. "Ma" Little was very much in evidence every day on that corner, as she and Hop lived in an upstairs apartment over Dodd's Garage, a few doors east of the grocery. We would see Ma making her rounds as she would come and go during the day. At that time, Hop was old and feeble and unable to walk. Their main source of income for years had been from keeping boarders. Hop had been an auctioneer in the

1920s and operated lunchrooms at 115 S. 5th and 429 Jefferson. Hop died in 1934. Ma had been an ironer at the Home Laundry and in her later years became a well known and loved community figure.

So well-known was Ma that her death and her story were printed in the Oct. 13, 1938 issue of the *Paducah News-Democrat*. The headline read, "Death comes to 'Ma' Little, who found happiness in devotion of her friends." The story is as follows:

Mrs. Rosalee Little, the little gray-haired lady who sold peanuts, candy and cold drinks downtown for more than a decade, despite her many years and slight feebleness due to age, was known to every Paducahan as "Ma" Little. In 1928 Ma, at age 59, was faced with the prospect of having to earn her own living. So she began selling peanuts on the corner. People became accustomed to seeing her there and began to like buying from the little, stooped, toothless woman who said, "Thank you, honey," to every customer. Her business flourished, as she made her way from door to door along the downtown streets. Soon she was able to buy a shiny pushcart and added candy and cold drinks to her stock. And in the summer months she also sold ice cream. She became a familiar figure, usually wearing a heavy tan dress and baseball cap as she made her rounds. She acquired many friends.

In 1936, T.O. Thomas, owner of Thomas Novelty Company, who had a number of vending machines around town, saw how much effort it was for Ma to push her heavy cart around and decided to lend a helping hand. He decided she should have her own store where she could continue to make her living, but more comfortably. Thomas discovered that many of Ma's friends were more than willing to help with this project, so they were able to have a store erected on property at 10th and Broadway owned by Edgar B. Fergerson. Workers from local labor unions gave their time and many Paducah businessmen donated the materials. Virtually every merchant made a contribution.

On Saturday morning May 30, 1936, Ma had her grand opening. It was the happiest day of her life. So great was her happiness and appreciation that she had a sign erected in front of the store which read, "My friends built this place for me." The store was a big success.

Her story was so humanly appealing that Jack Major, a Paducah vaudeville and radio star, presented it to radio producers, who promptly accepted it and invited Mrs. Little to New York, all expenses paid, to take part in the broadcast. T.O. Thomas accompanied her. The program was broadcast on Sunday afternoon Nov. 22, 1936. Many Paducahans were huddled near their radios to hear the program. Ma was as thrilled as a child and her voice was choked with emotion as it was broadcast coast to coast.

When Ma died, none of her friends were forgotten in her will. She left the store building to E.B. Fergerson, who had donated the property, and asked T.O. Thomas to distribute her estate to her benefactors.

Ma Little Store Site

West Kentucky Coal Tipple

Gathering Places and Gatherings

Hotel Irvin Cobb

The Irvin Cobb Hotel building holds a lot of fond memories for me, as it must for other Paducahans who were around in its heyday. When we first moved to Paducah in 1923, the only two places I knew were the Napoleon Apartments, where we lived, and my dad's grocery at 621 Broadway. This was four years before the Irvin Cobb Hotel was built. The 6th and Broadway site of the hotel was then the home of the Adolph Weil family. It was directly on the way from our home to my dad's store. I remember seeing Mr. and Mrs. Weil, then up in years, taking short daily walks in the neighborhood around the corner of 6th and Broadway.

By the time the Cobb was under construction, we had moved to Harahan Boulevard and Dad had moved the grocery to 10th and Broadway. I was at Tilghman High School on Murrell Boulevard, so I did not have many activities to take me to 6th Street downtown, so I have no recollection of the Cobb being built.

After I joined the Boy Scouts and remained active for over 16 years, I was well aware of the Cobb, as it was just across the street from Scout headquarters. And when I joined the Junior Chamber of Commerce, or Jaycees as they became known, I attended weekly Monday night meetings at the Cobb. One year, I was nominated for Jaycees president and my opponent was Bill Daily, manager of the hotel. (I withdrew my nomination as I knew the job required a lot of extra time that I did not feel I could take from work.)

When I joined the Rotary Club in 1956, it met every Wednesday at the Cobb. The club was forced to meet elsewhere for years when the hotel was closed due to a fire, until it was reopened. It still meets there each Wednesday.

Just before World War II, there was an annual March of

Dimes dance held in the lobby and ballroom of the hotel to raise money in support of the war effort. Also before and after the war, there were many dances at the Cobb, featuring famous dance bands. Dances were held on the roof in the summertime. The dances, usually held on weekends, were very popular and well attended and made the hotel the center of Paducah activity.

The hotel dining room on the lower level was always a popular place. Many businessmen ate there on weekdays. There was a large round table near the north end of the room that seated 10, who by their regular attendance, held an automatic reservation. They frowned if a stranger usurped one of the seats. Elihue Randolph was head waiter until the hotel was closed.

There was a beauty shop, barber shop and bar on the ground floor. Dumas Fields ran the barber shop and his wife operated the beauty shop. When my barber moved to the Cobb, I followed him and continued to go there until he left.

Several of my good friends worked at the Cobb. When I met Alvin Gupton he was one of the four bellhops. Other friends were Jess Carneal, who married June Lockwood and lived across from us on Vine Street, and Harry Devinney, who became the hotel manager. Margie Clements Gupton worked at the reception desk for many years. I later hired her as switchboard operator, when I was office manager at Petter Supply. She held that job until she retired many years later. Another long-time Petter employee was Pearl Day, whose husband, Carl, was night clerk at the Cobb for many years.

There was a pool hall in the basement. The only access was via the stairs down to the men's rest room. When you came into the building from the 6th Street entrance, the stairs were just past the bar on the right and just to the right of the stairs which led up to the mezzanine. One had to walk past a row of lavatories on the west wall to reach the door to the pool hall. Dexter Howell owned and operated the pool hall. He also was a partner of Tom "Buck" Willingham in the Cat & the Fiddle Restaurant on Broadway near 32nd Street.

The Palmer House Hotel

*T*he Palmer House was **the** hotel in the early 1920s. It was right in the center of all downtown activities, across from the post office and Elks Club and nestled among the five movie houses, the banks and stores. Within the hotel were the Gilbert-Bennett Drugstore on the 5th and Broadway corner, a barber shop, pool room and Boswell's Restaurant, considered the most prestigious place for dining. It had been the meeting place for the Rotary Club since the club was chartered in 1915. Rotary held its inaugural banquet in the Gold Ballroom, just off the lobby.

While in high school, two close friends, Paul Martin and Jeff Robinson, got jobs at the drugstore. Many of our schoolmates switched from Walker's Drugstore across the street, to give their Coke and sandwich business to Paul and Jeff. During the lunch hour, many students from St. Mary's School, two blocks away, came to the drugstore, as well. During the first few years I worked at Petter Supply Company on 1st Street, I walked there for lunch.

Another of my classmates, Jimmy Yeltema, became the night watchman at the Palmer House after graduation. He had an "office" in the basement which he outfitted with furniture, a radio, icebox and carpeting, so he could lounge, read and listen to music between his hourly rounds to the various punch stations.

Curtis Foy, who had his jewelry business in one of the buildings next to the Palmer House, was there until the hotel was demolished to make way for the J.C. Penney store. Foy's younger daughter, Martha Sue, married one of my close friends, Henry Ivey, who became an assistant to his father-in-law in the jewelry store. Henry and I ate breakfast regularly at Boswell's. Some evenings, he and I took Mr. Foy upstairs for a few games of pool before going home for dinner. The manager of the pool room was Leon Raper, who was manager at my father's main store until it was closed in 1933.

There was a large round table that seated eight on the upper level of Boswell's Restaurant, which became reserved space for a number of prominent businessmen, including my boss Stanley Petter. A stranger dared not occupy a chair at this table, for he would be told to move.

Palmer House Hotel, Fifth and Broadway

Although it was demolished over 40 years ago, memories of the elegance of the Palmer House remain alive for many old-time Paducahans. It was erected in 1892 at a cost of $125,000. It was named for Elbridge Palmer, then president of the City National Bank, who contributed $8,000 at a time when efforts to save its investors from abandoning plans to build it seemed about to fail.

The three-story red brick building which dominated the downtown at the northeast corner of 5th and Broadway, contained 114 rooms with baths on each floor, hydraulic passenger and freight elevators, steam heat and thorough ventilating facilities. It was described as "the most imposing architectural ornament in Paducah." It was common for traveling men to spend Sundays at the Palmer House in order to enjoy the dining and other facilities. Boswell's Restaurant, added later, increased the hotel's popularity and appeal.

Charles Reed, Proprietor of the Palmer House

Charles Reed, whose company built the Palmer House Hotel, was a self-made man. He was born in 1842 and after only a few years of public education, left school at the age of 12 and entered a tobacco factory as an apprentice. He served this trade until the outbreak of the Civil War.

Reed enlisted in the Third Regiment Breckinridge Division, under the command of Lloyd Tilghman. During his last three years of service, he was with General Nathan Bedford Forrest's division and was with him in all Forrest's celebrated raids throughout Kentucky and Tennessee.

At the end of the war in 1867, without funds, but with staunch friends, he joined John Segenfelter of Paducah in the ownership of the European Hotel at 107 S. 2nd St. The hotel became one of the most popular resorts in the city. In 1876, he purchased a half interest in the Richmond House at 1st and Broadway. It became the most popular hostelry in town. Reed then organized a stock company which built the Palmer House and was its proprietor for 16 years.

Reed married Jessie Woods, daughter of Captain Eliah Woods, in 1868. Their daughter Emma grew up in the Palmer House and married Ed Noble, brother of "Captain" Bob Noble. In a 1959 interview, she told Lucille McMurry, then women's editor of the *Sun-Democrat*, that living in the hotel in its heyday was wonderful.

Charles Reed was a city councilman for a number of years. He was elected Paducah mayor in 1881, served four successive two-year terms and it is said he inaugurated more improvements during his terms than had his predecessors in years. A paid fire department was established in 1882, replacing the valiant, though inadequate, volunteer fire-fighters. Also during his terms of office, the two-story city hall at 4th and Kentucky was built in 1883 at a cost of $20,000. Its basement served as jail quarters.

Woman's Club of Paducah

The Woman's Club of Paducah was organized on Nov. 15, 1906, and incorporated on Jan. 6, 1907. Three months later it joined the Kentucky Federation of Woman's Clubs.

The club was first located at 608 Kentucky Ave., in a house shown in the 1894-1895 city directory as the residence of Mrs. Anna Grief, widow of Martin J. Grief, a dealer in wallpaper, picture frames, moldings and paper hanging; and William S. Grief, a paper hanger. In the 1904 directory, the property was listed for L.A.M. Grief, paper hanger, a resident of 323 Jefferson.

The building was shown in 1908 as occupied by the Merchants Credit Rating Bureau, Miss Monnie O'Brien, secretary; Retail Merchants Association, James A. Rudy, president; J.A. Wolfe, vice president; W.E. Cochran, secretary and treasurer. There were 30 members and directors were Jacob Wallerstein, Harry Hank, William Rieke, Charles Weille and R.D. Clements.

The woman's club was the third occupant shown and in 1908, Mrs. James A. Rudy was president. In his 1927 book, *The Story of Paducah*, Fred Neuman lists the following club presidents: Mrs. J.A (Katie) Rudy, 1906 - 1912; Mrs. Elbridge (Mary G.) Palmer, 1912 - 1914; Mrs. Robert B. (Kate) Phillips, 1914 - 1916; Mrs. H.G. Wells, 1916 - 1918; Mrs. Roy (Mary) McKinney, 1918 - 1920; Mrs. H.J. (Elizabeth) Hills, 1920 - 1924; Mrs. T. Edgar (Virginia) Elgin, 1924 - 1927; and Mrs. C.E. Percell, 1927.

On Sept. 24, 1925, the clubhouse was enlarged and remodeled. That same year, my family moved from the Napoleon Apartments to the upstairs apartment of the Langstaff home at 715 Kentucky Ave., so I remember the clubhouse before and during the renovation. I was 11 years old and one of a number of neighborhood boys who went to the clubhouse on weekends when no one was there. Before the new construction began, we played in the flower garden in the backyard, which was kept nicely mowed and clean. A number of pieces of white marble-like statuary, some life-size, were placed among the flowers around the high wooden fence which enclosed the back. During the renovation, we roamed all over the building, going up to the second floor balcony and jumping over the railing onto a huge sand pile in front of the new stage being built on the first floor.

Between 1927 and 1937, there were a number of stage plays and concerts at 608 Kentucky while the woman's club was there. Dr. W.B. Washburn was a frequent master of ceremonies. I recall "H.M.S Pinafore," which was performed by local artists and I sang in the chorus and in the "Hornpipe" dance. A Mr. Mitchell sang the main vocal numbers. He had a beautiful high tenor voice and was the best talent in the show- when sober. We had three shows before packed houses and the first two went smoothly. The third was a nightmare. Mitchell did not show for the afternoon run-through for the Saturday night performance. He was finally located in a bar downtown - totally fall-down drunk. Several people spent hours filling him with black coffee, putting him into a cold shower and getting him in shape to sing. An hour before curtain, he was still in a stupor and kept wanting to go to sleep. His role did not require him to be on stage until midway through the first act, but we were all holding our breath, doubting if he could stand up, much less sing. When he made his appearance, we all breathed easier. The first three numbers went well, although he acted and sang as though in a trance. After the next curtain, he came to and with prompting from behind the curtain, struggled for the rest of the show. The audience was aware that he was hung over. Later, he acknowledged he had no memory of the first act and only realized he was on stage when he came to in the second act. Too bad there was no stand-in.

A local boy's club called the Von Barons, rented the woman's club ballroom for Friday night dances from 1931 to 1940.

The last year the woman's club was listed as an occupant at 608 Kentucky Ave., was 1937. The directory for 1939 lists the 608 address as the location of Draughon's Business College, J.B. Taylor, manager. During that time, I bought insurance from a fellow Jaycee member, Joseph Martin Lindsey McMahon, who was a salesman for the Penn-Mutual Insurance Company and married to Siddie Hassman. He then went to work for the college at 608 Kentucky.

Apparently, the woman's club moved its headquarters to the Irvin Cobb Hotel in 1937, or after. A 1947 directory shows Mrs. Lou Esther Manchester as president that year and the club still at the hotel. The club later moved to 1406 Jefferson, its present home, in August, 1957, in a home formerly owned by Ben Billings, who owned Billings Printing Company.

The former woman's club house on Kentucky was used between 1956 and 1966 for rehearsals for the Charity League Follies held every other year. For three weeks performers, I among them, crowded the upstairs front rooms for four hours Monday through Friday before the Follies. Dr. Raymond Roof then bought the old clubhouse, had it torn down and erected his dental office and practiced there for many years. Today it is the dental office for Robert Garey, where I go for regular checkups.

50th Anniversary Party for Irvin Cobb

One of the most notable events held at the Kentucky Avenue location of the Woman's Club of Paducah was the 50th anniversary party for one of Paducah's favorite sons, Irvin S. Cobb. This event was held on April 29, 1926, and attended by 300 people. Many others requested tickets, but were turned down because 300 was the maximum number the club could accommodate.

Cobb, born in Graves County in 1876, became managing editor of the *Paducah News* in 1895 at the age of 19. Later he wrote for New York City newspapers and the *Saturday Evening Post.* He did not begin to publish any of his writings until 1937.

The dinner, given under the auspices of the Paducah Rotary Club, began with welcoming remarks by Dr. O.B. Powell, Rotary president, followed by Toastmaster Elliott Mitchell, managing editor of the *Paducah Evening Sun.*

Mrs. Robert B. Phillips, a past president of the woman's club from 1914 to 1916, speaking on behalf of the women of Paducah, offered what was considered an eloquent tribute to Cobb. Other dignitaries at the speakers' table included Robert H. Davis of New York City, editor of *Munsey's Magazine,* a close friend of Cobb and frequent visitor to Paducah; and Fred Neuman, columnist and feature writer for the *Paducah Evening Sun* and author of several books on Cobb. A picture of those at this speakers' table now hangs in the upstairs lecture room of the Paducah Public Library.

Carnegie Library, Ninth and Broadway

The Von Baron Ironclad Fraternity

The idea of a boy's club was conceived in the fertile mind of Edwin Oscar Davis in 1931, my senior year in high school. I first knew Oscar when I lived in the Napoleon Apartments and the Davis family lived around the corner, on the south side of 6th between Washington and Clark. We first met at Robert Lee Grade School. We had a few classes together, but my only recollection of him there was the time I noticed his ability to draw pictures. We were making posters for a project and while mine and others were irregular and crude, Oscar's were excellent and looked almost professional. He could draw faces and bodies that looked like real people. I learned later that he was an avid reader of history and had a quick wit and sharp mind. We were not close friends until later and I saw little of him until we became members of the boy's club.

My brother Harry and I heard that a new boy's club was being formed and in only a few months of its existence, we were invited to join. The members then numbered about 12 and they had rented an upstairs room over an auto body shop behind the young men's tennis court at 715 Kentucky Ave. They met on Monday nights in a room with a single table and straight-back chairs.

Oscar was the mastermind behind the whole organization. He wrote the charter, devised the rules and regulations and order of governing. He became the first president and named the group the Von Baron Ironclad Fraternity and patterned it after the procedures and rules he had read about Prussian army methods. He made up special names and foreign-sounding titles for the officers. After 70 years I don't remember those, but think one officer was called Balmine.

Weekend dances

We finally had about 40 members, most of them former Tilghman High students. Most are gone now, many deceased and

92

I Remember Paducah When...

some living elsewhere. Among those still here are Ray Strittmatter, Harry Livingston and "Junior" Townsend. Our main activity was giving and attending weekend dances. Rarely a week passed that we didn't have a dance. We held many dances at the woman's club, next door to the Kentucky Avenue Presbyterian Church at 6th and Kentucky. A few were at the Odd Fellows Hall on the northeast corner of 5th and Kentucky and more formal dances were held at the Irvin Cobb and Ritz hotels. We also attended many out of town dances, mostly those at the Legion Hall in Mayfield. Those in Mayfield frequently booked big name bands, which attracted people from counties all around. Most local dances cost from $2 to $3 a couple, with stags about half that. There usually was a local band providing the music, led by Jack Stahlcup or Harry Ware, whose musicians held day jobs and made extra money playing in the bands on weekends.

All the dances we sponsored were chaperoned. We asked the mothers of the girls we dated to be chaperones for us. We always had three who sat together at the end of the dance floor to see to it there was no unruly behavior. They kept a watchful eye on the doors and made certain no couples left the room during the dance. Fortunately, this was before liquor was legal, so there was no drinking. Everyone came to dance.

Among the chaperones who served regularly were Mrs. G.W. Dunbar, Helen's and Bill's mother; Mrs. H.P. McElrath, Dorothy's mother; Mrs. Fred Lack, Beverly's mother; Mrs. John Polk, Martha's mother; Mrs. Ed Cave, Jane's mother; Mrs. Tuttle Lockwood, June's mother; and Mrs. Slavie Mall, Mary Ellen's mother

The dance floor was bare, with chairs placed around the walls for sitting and resting between dances. They were "break" dances, where couples could change partners and the boys who came without dates could "break" or cut in and dance with the girls. This was a good arrangement for all, as the stags could dance with all the girls and the girls could dance with boys other than their dates. A lot of us did not have cars and could not afford dates, so we benefited from that arrangement.

It was a club rule that we all saw to it that all the girls got to dance with many boys. The most popular girls were "broken" during every dance, while some were not so popular and would be stuck dancing with only their dates. When we saw this, we agreed to break in and dance with them. We had a secret sign to indicate we wanted to be "broken." Since we danced cheek to cheek, the girls were not aware of the sign and not embarrassed.

Benny Lookoffsky, one of our later members, financed a number of our dances. He hired musicians or had a jukebox and charged 99 cents a couple or stag.

The Dunbars

As the club membership grew, we lived in all parts of town, so decided we needed a more central meeting location. A lot of the members either worked at or hung around Dunbar's Drugstore, on the corner of 17th and Broadway. The Dunbars owned a small house behind the store on South 17th Street, which they rented, so when it became vacant, they rented it to us, probably to get us away from cluttering up the front door of the drugstore. Since we owned no furniture, moving presented no problem, but as our new place had several rooms, we needed sofas, chairs, tables and lamps. We all scrounged what we could from our homes and the Dunbars helped us enough to make the place look fairly furnished. We looked upon the Dunbars as our mentors, although as some of our misdeeds and pranks surfaced, I am sure they would admit to no relationship other than landlord.

Still later, we needed more room, as we could not get all members together in one room for meetings. We rented a large three-story frame building on the corner of 23rd and Broadway, across the street from the Ritz Hotel. The previous owner had remodeled the house from a residence to a funeral home, but closed it after a few years. The downstairs front rooms were spacious and well-suited to our needs. We put what furniture we had in the rooms, bought several ping-pong tables and got two pool tables and put them in the large upstairs rooms. Soon our clubhouse became a most popular place, with many members stopping by every day.

Since it was midtown, it was convenient to stop by going to and from downtown. We were surrounded by residences, so had to post rules to keep down the noise and boisterous behavior, for fear of protests from our neighbors.

No jackets in school

We wanted jackets with emblems on the backs to give us more identity. As usual, Oscar came up with a design. He sketched a pair of eagle's wings with a knight's helmet on top and a shield for the body. The jackets were dark blue corduroy with each member's name stitched on the front.

We were excited when these jackets were distributed at a meeting and agreed we would wear them to school the next day. When we showed up in the first morning class, we all were summoned, one at a time, to report immediately to Principal Walter C. Jetton's office. He gave each of us a stern lecture, told us to remove our jackets immediately and not to wear them to school or at school. We were certain that Jetton had heard of us, and apparently, what he heard was not good. Fraternities were not permitted in high school, as they were considered disruptive and divisive and a problem creator. Because I was a member of the club, it affected my grades to some extent and probably knocked me out of any chance of being considered for the Honor Society.

Last clubhouse

Our last clubhouse was built out on the Blandville Road, about a quarter of a mile this side of the Angles, the Langstaff summer home. The lot was owned by the Dunbars and we built a one-room one-story frame barn-like house near the back of the lot, which sloped down from the highway for about 100 feet. We all pitched in and made a gravel road entrance. Oscar was our architect and construction foreman and designed the rectangular structure, which had a long side parallel to the road. I don't remember if we had an outhouse or inside plumbing. I do remember we had a stove for heat. Compared to our clubhouse on 23rd Street, it was very primitive. We had less than a third of the space, but we were out in the country, away from other people and could whoop and holler all we wanted.

This clubhouse, our last, was not used as much as had our others, probably due to its location and partly due to the fact that some members had gone to college, some moved away and some were married or just lost interest. It was used primarily for the weekly meetings or on weekends, seldom during the week. Members got out of the habit of stopping by. There was usually a crap game going on during the weekends by a small bunch who had the money and liked to gamble.

One project we had while at the Blandville clubhouse was building a sailboat. There again, Oscar was the one who got it started and drew the plans. We bought the materials and had them delivered to the club site. We worked on the boat many hours after work and on weekends. It took all of one summer. When finished, it was a monstrous-looking craft and extremely heavy.

We had it loaded onto a big flatbed truck one member borrowed, and on a Sunday afternoon, hauled it right down Broadway to the Ohio River. We had several problems en route, as the mast was not hinged or removable and we had to be careful not to get it tangled with overhead wires. But, finally, we made it. Many of us rode in the back and we attracted a lot of curious looks by people we passed, who probably wondered what this strange contraption was doing on Paducah's main street. I doubt if we applied for a permit, or at least, we didn't have one. No one questioned us and there were no repercussions.

We wondered if the boat would float and if it did, would it stay upright. To our relief, all went well. Since Kentucky Lake was then some years away, we had to use the Ohio River, not the best place for a sailboat due to the current and the relatively narrow channel.

A memory now

I don't remember how or when we disbanded. We just faded away. It could have happened when Oscar moved to Louisville. He put himself through law school and became a very successful practicing attorney and built a beautiful home on the banks of the Ohio River, east of downtown Louisville.

What was at one time an alive, active and close-knit group of teenagers, bonded together by common interests and a secret code of loyalty to each other and a pledge of everlasting friendship, is now a fond and fading memory. We rubbed shoulders with all types of boys, similar but diverse - weak and strong, big and little, loud and quiet, aggressive and placid, motivated and indifferent, mean and kind, comical and serious, leaders and followers, rich and poor, givers and takers. We learned whether to go along with the crowd or resist peer pressure and decline to participate in any activity that offended our sense of right. It was not always easy. I did some things I regret, but on balance, I treasure the experience I had as a member and feel that what I gained from that period of growing up has been a help to me in many ways.

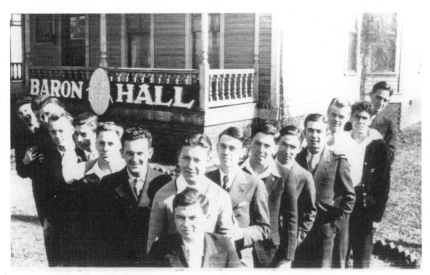

Baron Hall, 23rd and Broadway, 1933
Left to Right-Owen Cummings, Frank Trevathan, Charles Sills, Chat Rhodes,
Barron White, Charles Humphries, John Wright Polk, Tom Vaughn, Marvin
Scyster, Harry White, Ernest Mitchell, Edgar Edwards, Ellis Rives, Taftman
Abernathy and Gus Singleton

Wonderful Neighborhoods

Harahan Boulevard

*I*n 1928, our dad opened his number three store on the corner of 16th and Harrison streets. The family moved from Kentucky Avenue to the 300 block of North 15th Street, now named Harahan Boulevard, after a president of the Illinois Central Railroad.

Most of the residents of that five-block-long street were employees of the railroad, as were the residents of many other nearby streets within walking distance of the railroad shops on Kentucky Avenue. We soon became acquainted with the children in the neighborhood. Betty and Helen Cooley, who lived across the street, were daughters of Ryan Cooley, an ICRR conductor, as were the fathers of John Mercer, Roby Robertson and Jack Baker. George Denker was a special agent, meaning he walked passenger and freight cars, catching people who rode the rails free.

Dr. Harry Abell Sr. lived on the corner from us, Lee Powell's father-in-law, Ralph Scott, was a neighbor, as well. J.H. Martin and children, Jewel, Josephine, Jim and Tom, lived in the next block, as did the John Polk family, Martha, John Wright Jr. and Barbara. Laura Margaret and Martha Sue Foy, daughters of Curtis Foy of Foy's Jewelers, were two blocks away. Others our age were Joe and John Wilson, Tommy Phipps, "Ate" and Boyce Moodie-both of whom starred in football at Tilghman, - Bill Feiler and Jenrose Weedman.

We enjoyed that neighborhood, within walking distance of school and only a block from Dad's store.

Harahan Hoboes

 e called ourselves the "Harahan Hoboes." We were more than a dozen high school age boys living on or around Harahan Boulevard. After school and on weekends, we gathered around the corner at Harrison Street or hung out at Rip Seamon's grocery at the corner of Clay Street. We played touch football on one of the vacant lots or "horse" or one-on-one basketball games in the alley behind one of the boy's homes. We occasionally roamed the neighborhood streets, played tennis on the nearest court, which was on Fountain Avenue, or congregated on the front porch of one of the neighborhood girl's homes.

During summer evenings, a number of us occasionally walked to the river where it was cool. The Illinois Central Railroad spur track ran from the freight depot at 6th and Campbell down to the river, where it curved behind old Riverside Hospital, paralleled the river and continued on First Street over to the NC&St.L freight depot. Along the river, the track ran over a 400-foot wooden trestle constructed about 30 feet above a large hollow used for years as a city dump. People hauled their trash, old worn-out appliances and broken furniture - even a few old automobiles - and dumped them over the edge. Old cardboard cartons and newspaper were everywhere. You could not see much of what was below, for the hollow had been overgrown with weeds for years. There was no landfill in those days and all refuse was left where it fell.

One night, a group of us decided to go to the trestle and walk the rails and play our game of vying to see who could stay on longest without falling off. The height above the hollow made the game more hazardous and challenging. After a while, we tired of that and sat on the rails about midway and began swapping stories. One of the older boys pulled out a pack of cigarettes and offered them around. Several took one and fired up. We were there almost an hour when we heard the nightly train approaching. Soon the train's searchlight lighted up the area, so we decided we had better head for the higher ground. Those who were smoking flicked their cigarettes over the side and ran. By the time we reached high ground, the engine was already on the trestle. We jumped off the tracks onto the grass and stayed there until the engine, its four cars and caboose went by.

It was then that we noticed a large blaze in the middle of the dump. In no time it became a huge fire, with flames reaching upward, lighting up the sky. Then we began to hear the rumble of fire trucks and their sirens screeching into the night, becoming louder as they approached the area. To put it mildly, we were a scared bunch of boys. We hurriedly decided we should not panic and run, which would attract attention to us. So we decided to split up and each take a separate route back and meet at Harahan.

The next morning there was a big article about the fire on the front page of the *Paducah News-Democrat* and a statement that all fire trucks in town were called out and that the firemen fought the blaze all night. The headline read, "Hoodlums set fire to city dump."

West Broadway Homes

In the 1930s, there were a number of fine homes on Broadway, west of 28th Street. A few remain, but most are gone. On the northwest corner was a home owned by the Fred Lack family. Fred was owner of Lack Wholesale Grocers Company at 3rd and Jefferson. He had previously owned the Lack Singletree Company, and was a partner in several other companies in the early 1900s. Mrs. Lack (Genevieve) was a very pretty, vivacious and elegant lady, whose charming personality endeared her to everyone, especially the young people she frequently invited to parties at her home. Fred was a courteous, dignified gentleman, but also outgoing and friendly. Their eldest child, Beverly, at 16, was one of the town beauties. She had a smile for everyone and was very popular. Fred Jr., at 14, was friendly, but shy. The younger son, Buddy, was six and seldom stayed around when the family had company.

The Lack property faced Broadway with a backyard fence enclosing a tennis court on the southwest corner of Jefferson. The court was kept busy all day by both serious tennis players and those more interested in Beverly. My brother Harry and I were interested both in tennis and Beverly, but realized there was too much competition for Beverly's attention, so confined our interest to tennis. We were considered good dancers and were occasionally invited to the Lack parties.

Next door, west of the Lack home, was the residence of Robert Reeves, president of the People's Bank. The two-story brick home featured a wide front porch with several white columns. The children, two boys and a girl, were younger than we were. After Robert's death, the home was demolished and the property acquired by the Broadway Church of Christ for a parking lot.

The only other prominent house on the north side of that block was the Mallory home, one of the first homes built in the west end. This frame house was known for its peculiar front steps, one side short and the other long. They were built at an angle which made them appear to face one way until you went past, then to face the other way. When the house was demolished, the steps were saved and stored in the backyard of the Alben Barkley Museum at 5th and Madison.

Mrs. Mallory was the daughter of Dr. Sam Caldwell, who was president of the West End Improvement Company, which owned and developed the block. The Mallory place was sold to the American Legion and later demolished to make way for the People's Bank West End Branch, which is still there.

There were two historic homes on the south side of that block. A two-story brick with white columns, somewhat similar to the Reeves' home, was the honeymoon home for the Saunders Fowlers. Behind the house was the Edgewood Dairy, considered "out in the country" in the early days. The home was later purchased by Dr. Robert W. "Red" Robertson. His widow, Helen, lives there at this time. The dairy is long gone, but the dairy barn is still there and used as a garage and shed.

The other historic home was owned by the Leo Keiler family. A fire destroyed the original structure, but it was rebuilt. It was recently demolished and the property acquired by the First Baptist Church, which was in the next lot on the west side.

So, what was a nice, beautiful residential block outside the city limits, which had a lot of large oak trees, is now occupied by two churches, a bank, the West Branch Post Office and an investment firm.

Fountain Avenue

Since the early 1900s, Fountain Avenue has been one of the finest residential neighborhoods in the city. It was one of only two boulevards in the west end with medians, the other being Jefferson Street, beyond 19th.

There were a number of old-time, well-known Paducah families who lived in the blocks from Broadway to Lang Park. The two-story red brick house at 113 Fountain was impressive, having three large white columns, a full-length front porch and two balconies on the second floor. It was the home of several prominent Paducah families. L.S. Dubois, owner of the Dubois Wholesale Drug Company, lived in the house in the early 1900s. James H. Rudy of the Rudy Department Store, lived there for a number of years. The Rudys sold the place to Dr. W.C. Eubanks, a local physician, who lived there until his death.

Our family moved into the Eubanks house in 1933, a few months after I was employed by the Petter Supply Company. We lost our N. 25th Street home after the death of my father earlier the same year. Adelaide Eubanks, who was in my high school graduating class, married Hal Houston, a young doctor from Murray and moved there. Mrs. Eubanks married a retired California senator named Piles. After they tied the knot, he continued to live in California and she stayed in Paducah. Local gossip was that each thought the other was wealthy and apparently, neither was.

We lived there seven years, were there during the flood of 1937 and moved away in 1940, when Harry and I bought a small cottage on Friedman Avenue. We loved the place on Fountain. It was convenient, being midtown, where we could get everywhere we wanted to be in a few minutes. A lot of our friends lived within

Our home, 1933-1940 at 113 Fountain Ave

walking distance. During the past 10 years, we have been distressed to see it vacant and slowly deteriorating. We are delighted to see that Fred and Marta Vowell of Painter's Supply have bought the property and have renovated the house and will make it their home.

129 Fountain Ave, built by the Sherrill family.

A 50-plus-year Career

Getting a Job

In the summer of 1933, the family stores were closed and I had been looking for a job for more than a week, when I was invited to visit friends at Murray College. I decided to hitchhike there and spend the day. I put on a pair of knee-length knickers, because I wanted to look like a young boy, as it was easier to hitch a ride. I stood on the corner of 21st and Park Avenue, by

Petter Supply, 117 - 119 South First Street, 1933

Andrew Jackson School, to thumb a ride.

Soon I was picked up by R.B. Phillips, a real estate agent. When I told him I needed a job, he said I should apply at Petter Supply Company, which was owned by his son-in-law, Stanley Petter. He said Mr. Petter had told him the company was going to hire two men. Mr. Phillips let me out at 6th and Kentucky and I thought I would go on to Murray and apply at Petter Supply the next day. I tried for about 30 minutes to thumb a ride, without success. I kept thinking about that job and decided I had better go apply right away and forget about going to Murray.

Mr. Petter was very gracious and made me feel at ease. He asked a number of questions, then escorted me on a tour of the warehouse. When we returned to his office, he told me he would put me on the payroll and that I should report for work at 7 a.m. the following morning. As I got up to leave, he said, "I suggest you not wear your knickers, but get some long pants."

Introduction to the Industrial Supply Business

The country was still in the midst of the Depression in 1933, when I began working at the Petter Supply Company. Many people were not able to find jobs and I felt lucky to have one. The new National Recovery Act (NRA) required employers to observe a 40-hour work week and that is what opened up the opportunity for me to be hired. I knew nothing about the industrial supply business, having worked only for my father in his grocery stores and having had a morning paper route for the *Paducah News-Democrat*. I didn't know a peavy from a pike pole and knew nothing about pipe fittings - that they came with male and female threads. I learned that a nipple was a short piece of pipe threaded on both ends. I had to learn there was a difference between a machine bolt and a carriage bolt and that a cap screw was made in either national coarse of SAE automotive fine threads. But the experience opened up a new world to me.

In the course of my 50-plus years of working there, I obtained a broad knowledge of industry and production in this country and abroad. I got to travel five states - Kentucky, Tennessee, Illinois, Missouri and Arkansas - and got to make calls on customers and suppliers whose main offices and plants were in the large metropolitan cities of St. Louis, Chicago, Boston, Cincinnati and Pittsburgh. This included calls on all types of companies - coal, clay and fluorspar, mines, rock quarries, steel mills, foundries, marine vessels and manufacturing plants of every description.

I've gone underground in a coal mine, descended into the vertical shaft of a fluorspar mine and spent half a day crawling around the inside of a large steam boiler, handing firebrick and asbestos fire wall lining material to our crew of installers at a coal mine in Harrisburg, Ill.

I remember a few occasions in those early years when I goofed up. Once I stepped into a sand mold at Jackson Foundry after Charley Jackson had spent several hours shaping it for a special casting. And I recall a summer Saturday afternoon when I had to deliver a barrel of coal tar pitch to Paducah Cooperage Company, out on Myers Street on the bank of the Tennessee River. The barrel was loaded onto my pickup at the store, but when I got to the plant, I couldn't find anyone to help me unload. I kicked the chock out from under and rolled it off the back end. When it hit, the bung fell out and as it was hot weather, about half the contents spilled out onto the ground before I could roll the bung to the high side.

On another Saturday, I delivered a coil of two-inch manila rope, weighing more than 300 pounds, to Igert's Fleet on the Tennessee River. Again, I could not find anyone to help me unload, so I backed the truck down the slope and rolled the rope off on the river bank. As luck would have it, instead of landing on a flat side, it rolled down the bank, hit the gangplank and fell over into the river. I walked up the gangplank to the office, which was on a floating barge, and asked Earl Curtis, the bookkeeper and office manager, to sign my ticket. When he asked me where I put the rope, I told him it was just outside about 15 feet away.

Paducah Riverfront, 1950s

First Years in the Petter Office

After working in the shipping department, on the front sales counter and driving the city delivery truck during my first years at Petter Supply, owner and general manager Stanley Petter summoned me to his office. He said he was dissatisfied with how filing was being done and wanted me to take over the job from long-time sales employee Roland Hale, who worked the front counter and had been doing the filing early in the morning before he went to his counter and the job he enjoyed. The files and file cabinets were a mess and I was instructed to improve the system. I was to come into the office first to file, and go to my job in the shipping department, which was headed by Forrest Tincher. I did this for the first part of each day and within several weeks, had the cabinets and files in good condition. Mr. Petter was so pleased he asked me to come to the office on a full-time basis.

My first job in the office was to periodically write each supplier to keep pricing information up to date. I was put in charge of the cost file, which was the loose-leaf 800-page Petter Blue Book, which the company published periodically. Until I was drafted to serve in the Army in 1942, I was also involved in quoting on inquiries received from out-of-town accounts. Sales personnel gave me lists of items to quote and indicate what profit to add. Each year the company spent the entire month of December taking inventory. And whenever it was decided to publish a new catalog, all office and sales personnel were involved, from Stanley Petter on down. This took from six months to a year to put together. I worked from 8 a.m. to 5 p.m. and punched a time clock as required by the NRA. Still another part of my job was to keep the shelves of manufacturers' catalogs, other books and binders, in order, with information always current.

We had two typists and they answered the telephone. Since there was no switchboard, all incoming calls were transferred by a series of long and short bell signals, with each key person assigned a code signal. Some of the old wooden bank furniture which must have been in use in the 1890s, when the building was a bank, was still in the office and in use until the 1937 flood.

I was given a very small room behind the main office. It had been the office of Henry A. Petter, who founded the company in 1890 and died in 1933, three months before I was hired.

Stanley Dubois Petter

Climbing the Ladder

When I returned to Petter Supply in 1945, I found my job had been given to Bob Rogers, so I was assigned to call on new prospective accounts within a 100-mile radius. During the years I traveled this route, we added 600 new accounts. While making calls in Madisonville in 1948, I learned by phone that three employees had left the company to go into business for themselves and that Stanley Petter wanted me to take over the department they had headed.

As once scarce materials became more plentiful, we saw we needed more frequent coverage of accounts. The area I covered was so large I got around only once every two months, so my territory was split into four areas, Kentucky, Tennessee, Illinois and Missouri, and a new salesman was hired for each area. I was in charge of these four men and responsible for holding monthly sales meetings and deciding marketing strategies. This was my assignment for a number of years.

I was happy to be part of the management team and on the sales-producing side of the company. Petter Supply had grown from about 18 employees to a force of more than 50. I no longer had to punch the time clock. I had a key to the office and store, knew the combination to the safe, was authorized to sign checks and in charge of hiring office employees. I was also in charge of buying office supplies and equipment and sat in on manager's meetings with Stanley Petter and Sam Locke, the store manager. In 1956, I was proposed for Rotary Club membership by Stanley Petter, who was a club past president. The company paid my dues. I was furnished a car for making outside calls and had the privilege of using it full time with all expenses paid by the company. Also in 1956, the company paid for me to attend a one-month seminar at the Harvard Business School in Boston. It was attended by more than 50 other distributor owners and managers from all over the country.

So I felt I had arrived. Our sales team held its own with the other teams and proved to be productive. As the company continued to grow, the office was expanded twice to cover new employees. The industrial group was divided into special sales teams and managers were named to head them. Other departments were added to handle personnel, payroll, purchasing and all the necessary government forms.

By 1980, the office and sales force was spread around and working in cubicles. Each team covered its own area of customers

Petter Supply Employees, 1950

and category of products. Instead of being part of the management team, I was a department head. Two of the four outside salesmen on our team had retired, one died and the other was covering more territory. I worked past the customary retirement age of 65 and continued in the same capacity until I retired in 1989 at 75.

Edison Dictating Machines

*D*on Williams, who had been Stanley Petter's right-hand man for years, suffered a stroke and was hospitalized about a week before the 1937 flood and I was told to handle Don's desk until he returned or a replacement was hired.

This was quite a challenge for me, substituting for Mr. Petter's number two man. There were six of us in the office in close quarters and I was conscious that my boss could hear every phone call I made or received. But Mr. Petter was patient and only now and then would comment or offer advice or suggestions to make me feel comfortable.

I had experience in handling correspondence, so had no difficulty dictating to Don's secretary. Mr. Petter dictated into a machine, a dictaphone, and his stenographer waited until afternoon, put on her earphones and transcribed his letters. About a month after I took over Don's desk, Mr. Petter suggested I use the dictaphone which was on my desk. I was reluctant at first, but after a while I began and soon with his continued encouragement, was able to use the dictaphone without any problem.

A dictating machine is a wonderful time saver. You can use it for long letters, short ones, write a few now, stop for phone calls or other interruptions and put your thoughts on at intervals all day long. Then your secretary can transcribe at her convenience.

We had two Edison machines, which used wax cylinders which were about three inches in diameter and six inches long. Each

*Edison Dictating
Machine, 1933*

cylinder held about 10 to 15 average-length letters, after which it could be put into a shaver which erased the messages and the cylinder reused. A cylinder could be shaved until the wax was down to the core. We kept about a dozen cylinders on hand and the "girls" waited until all had been used and shaved them all at one time.

The dictating machine itself was contained in a black metal box about four inches wide, 12 inches long and a foot tall, with a short length of bright metal flexible tubing and a black mouthpiece. It had an adjustment for speed and volume. The shaver was mounted on a metal box with four casters. It stood about two feet high and had a horizontal motorized spindle for holding the cylinders to be shaved. We used these for years and they were sturdy and reliable with good fidelity. Around 1950, when the office was enlarged and new equipment purchased, the old wax machines were replaced with new electronic equipment.

CCC *Camp* 3560

Eighty thousand Kentuckians were enrolled in the Civilian Conservation Corps (CCC), established in 1933, to recruit millions of out-of-work people into a peacetime army of public works and conservation workers during the Depression. CCC Camp 3560 was established in Paducah in 1935 and was in operation until 1942, when the program was phased out. The camp was located at the west end of Clay Street, between what is now 23rd to 27th streets. At the time, the surrounding area was low and swampy, densely wooded and there were few residences.

I was working at Petter Supply Company when the camp was built and remember the camp people coming in to purchase materials and that we also made deliveries to them at the camp. Douglas Rose, who was employed at the time by the Soil Conservation Service, a part of the Department of Agriculture, spent most of his time at the camp and was in our office and sales department almost weekly buying various tools and supplies for the camp. When I returned from the Army in 1945 the camp was gone.

CCC 3560 Work Crews

Rotary Club

he Rotary Club of Paducah has been a big part of my life. It is a coincidence that the club was organized in 1914, the year I was born. I became a member in 1956 and have been active in the club since.

I first became aware of Rotary when my father became a member in 1924 and took me to one of the meetings, which were held at the Palmer House Hotel. My next experience came while a member of the Tilghman High School Glee Club. We sang at a meeting at the Irvin Cobb Hotel in 1931.

I was Stanley Petter's guest during his 1938-'39 presidency. In 1956, Mr. Petter sponsored me, when he became a senior active member, and I took his classification of industrial supplies. I was the 1971-'72 president and a few years later was named a Paul Harris Fellow, Rotary's highest honor. Paul Harris founded Rotary in 1903.

After my year as president, on my suggestion, a history committee was established and I was appointed to the committee. In 1980, the committee, comprised of Dick Fairhurst, Nat Dortch and me, published the first Rotary history.

While putting the history together I discovered that of the 55 charter members in 1915, I knew 30 personally or by sight. All were active in business and involved in civic activities.

During my working years as a member of Rotary with an active classification, I attended a number of district conferences, state conventions and one international convention in Hawaii.

Rotary has enriched my life and influenced me in many ways. I treasure the membership I still hold after many years, which include 20 with perfect attendance.

Exciting Times

The 1937 Flood

That Friday morning in January, 1937, when we went to work, the water was almost level with the foot of Broadway at 1st Street. It was predicted that the river would continue to rise, but how much higher was not known. Our entire staff began stacking what merchandise we could to a level higher than 53 feet, which was the highest water had ever reached before. In the front sales room, were several rows of 100-pound kegs of nails and washers which we stacked three or four high. In the office, we put some of the desks on top of others and took out the drawers of the wall files and stacked them on top. We thought we would be several feet above the water's eventual crest. Little did we know that the river would eventually cover the room within a few feet of the ceiling and that all our work would be for naught.

By 4:30 in the afternoon, the office and front sales room were completely surrounded by water, the center of the block being higher than the surrounding area. The driveway between the Petter building and Anderson's Blacksmith Shop was several feet deep in water, as was Maiden Alley in the rear of the building. It was getting dark and the current was too swift and hazardous to be waded. We telephoned the civil defense office at the fire station and were told they would dispatch two skiffs and haul us to high ground.

About 12 of us were standing at the back landing when they rowed up Maiden Alley from Kentucky Avenue. They loaded us in and gave us a paddle and all headed down the alley to Broadway and began rowing west. When the first boat reached 2nd Street on the east side of the Market House, they saw that the current was very swift and all were told to, "paddle like hell," and try to clear the intersection. The first boat didn't make it and was swept down North 2nd Street. I was in the second boat with Stanley Petter, who told us to start paddling fast and furiously before we hit 2nd Street and we were able to get through the intersection, although our boat was swept up to the front of Michael Hardware. We didn't capsize, though, and continued on Broadway until we got to 4th Street, under the Citizen's Bank clock, and were able to step out onto high ground. Stanley Petter had parked his car uptown and he took me to my home at 17th and Broadway, after which he was able to avoid the low spots that were flooded and reach his home in Avondale.

Looking east from 4th and Broadway, 1937 flood

Living in Lone Oak During the Flood

When the 1937 flood hit Paducah, our family was living in an upstairs apartment at the Eubanks home at 113 Fountain Ave. I lived with my mother and sister, both named Edna, and my brother Harry. My maternal great-aunt Sarah "Sadie" Vickers happened to be visiting us from Clarksburg, West Virginia, at the time. Sister Edna was dating Bob Sanderson, a Lone Oak resident and reporter for the *Paducah Sun-Democrat*.

The flood, which began to overflow downtown Paducah on Friday was about six feet deep in our yard by Sunday. We had been house-bound since Saturday morning, going out that day only once to wade around in the neighbor's yard trying to scrounge wood and coal to burn in our fireplaces.

Over the weekend, our utilities were being cut off one by one. First water flooded the basement, shut down the furnace and cut off our heat. We soon lost our phone, electric power and gas, which operated our water heater and stove. By Sunday morning, we were pretty well ready to vacate, but had no plan to do so. We thought the water might recede in a few days and we could ride it out. We were going to wait and see.

Late Sunday evening, Bob came by in a rowboat he had maneuvered through the front door and up to the second stair step to our apartment. He said he would take us to his home in Lone Oak for the duration. We talked it over and decided it was a good idea to leave. All, that is, but Aunt Sadie, who said she would stay in the apartment. Nothing we could say would change her mind, so we packed a few things and all but Aunt Sadie left with Bob, who rowed us out to the water's edge near 28th and Broadway, where he had parked his car. We went to his house where we four were given two rooms to use. We stayed there for almost four weeks until the water receded and we could get back into our apartment.

Monday morning, Harry and I caught a ride to 32nd and Broadway and with many others, helped unload food and other items that were brought in to Paducah by truck, boat and every other available means. By then, it was predicted that the flood would not be of short duration, but would be with us for weeks, so we began to be concerned for Aunt Sadie. We decided to row there and try to get her out. I walked to the makeshift dock that had been constructed across the 28th and Broadway intersection and saw there were a number of flat boats tied up, apparently left there by others after bringing families to high ground. Another man and I took one and rowed down into town, stopping first at my house.

Three hundred foot long dock at 28th and Broadway, 1937 flood

My aunt was sitting in a rocking chair by the front window and although she said she wanted to stay, I could tell she was ready to move. I told her I would be back and to pack her things. I then rowed with the man to his house on Monroe near 15th Street and waited while he searched his place. He found the house empty and no one around, so back we went to my apartment to pick up Auntie. By then, she was packed and ready to go. We made the trip without incident and got her settled at the Sandersons.

For three weeks, Harry and I worked at Bob's dad's grocery, waiting on customers and helping out with the expanded Lone Oak population, which had doubled or tripled during the crisis.

Around the first week in February, I received word that Stanley Petter wanted me to set up a flood office at his residence. I continued to stay at the Sandersons' and reported for work at the Petter home. We started by writing or phoning all our main factory sources, asking them to send us new catalogs and prices. We had stationery printed in Mayfield headed, "Temporary flood office," and as soon as we could obtain our ledger sheets from the safe, which had been under water, we wrote all customers and mailed current information to them. When we got our submerged files, we dried papers by spreading them on the terrazzo floor of the Petter den. Around the end of February, we were able to get back into our home and office and resume regular schedules.

Flying Lessons

bout the time there was talk of the United States enter-
ing the war against Germany, the government announced
the opportunity for young men to learn to fly. The
Civilian Pilot Training Program (CPTP) was offered in Paducah for
50 applicants to compete for 50 hours of free flight instruction. Ten
were to be chosen from those who scored the highest grades after two
weeks of ground instruction, given by Lt. Dick Devania, an Army
pilot from Paducah. I had always been interested in flying and wanted to learn, so I signed up for the class. I also persuaded my brother Harry to try out. We both made the final 10 and started taking
lessons from instructor L.E. "Toogie" Galbraith in Oct. 23, 1940.

At that time, the Paducah airport was at Howell Field, located on the Coleman Road, midway between Route 60 and Old Cairo
Road. The runways were short and the field small, but suitable for
the few privately-owned planes that used the field. There were no
commercial flights in or out of Paducah. And by odd coincidence,
Howell Field is now the site for the new Petter Supply Company
warehouse and office.

We 10 each took a 30-minute lesson every weekday morning. My time was 8:30 and Harry's was 10:30. I got back to the
Petter office from my lesson about 9:30 and Harry walked over from
his job at the International Shoe warehouse at 2nd and Jefferson and
picked up our car to go to his. He asked what instruction we had
that morning and I told him what happened.

After eight hours of instruction, the entire class soloed right
on schedule with no problems. Each day thereafter, we had a 15-
minute ride with the instructor and 15 minutes of soloing. Every
day we were taught new tactics - takeoffs and landings, climbs and
glides, cross-wind landings, cross controls, figure eights, pylon turns,
slipping and power off and power on stalls and spins.

On the first day for stalls and spins, Harry and I were a little apprehensive, for we thought this would be the most severe test so far. It turned out to be the simplest and easiest one to date. When Harry came to get the car later that morning and asked about it, I told him it was easy.

"You climb to 6,000 feet altitude, line up with Route 60 headed west and when you get to the cross road at Olivet Church Road, pull the throttle back to idle, pull the stick back into your stomach and let it start to stall. When it does, kick left rudder and let it spin. Then when you have completed two full 360 degree spins, push the stick forward and the plane will level off. Then climb back to 6,000 feet, do the same thing, but this time, kick right rudder. Then pull out after two 360 degree full turns."

When we got home after work that evening, we discussed the flying for the day and agreed we performed to our satisfaction. However, the next day when I arrived for my lesson, Toogie said to me, "Your brother almost gave me a heart attack yesterday." He said he watched as Harry climbed to altitude, then stalled and spun left. He said the plane kept spinning and spinning, until it disappeared behind the trees. He braced himself for a loud explosion or a ball of fire behind the trees, but said in a minute he saw the plane climbing back to altitude for another spin. Again, after it started stalling, this time to the right, he saw it spin and spin until again it went below the tree line. He waited a few minutes and again the plane climbed and then headed back to the field. He asked Harry why the long spin and Harry said, "I thought you were supposed to get it spinning good before you started counting."

Remembered Parks

E.H. Harriman Park

rom my desk at Petter Supply, I could see a grass plot on the river side of 1st Street, which was on the south side of the Armour Packing Company plant on Broadway, over to Kentucky Avenue. This was before the flood wall was built in 1940. I didn't know until I retired and began researching Paducah history that the plot was and for many years had been, an official city park.

The park was a very popular and busy place most of the year, as many citizens came to the river front regularly to watch the activity on the water. The old Fowler wharf boat was still anchored at the foot of Broadway and there were always commercial and pleasure craft that stopped to tie up for a short time. In the summertime, it was a favorite spot for a few local preachers, who occupied the space to "spread the Word" to anyone who would listen. They showed up with their soft leather, gilt-edged Bibles to talk about the Scriptures. I remember two barbers, who had shops on lower Broadway, who went when their business was slow in the afternoon. One of them was dubbed "Paul the Apostle." They discussed (translated that means argued) various passages of the Bible and they always had a large audience, including some hecklers. Around 4 p.m., the crowd would disperse and the barbers returned to their shops.

This grass plot was officially named E.H. Harriman Park. It was named for Edward Henry Harriman, who made his fortune in investments and took over the bankrupt Union Pacific Railroad. At the time of his death, he controlled more than 60,000 miles of railroads, including a major stock holding in the Illinois Central. His son, W. Averell Harriman, was better known, as he was active in government in the 1940s and served in the Roosevelt administration. He was once governor of New York and served as U.S. ambassador to Great Britain and later to Russia.

Bob Noble Park

or the first six years or so that we lived in Paducah, Bob Noble Park meant very little to me and my family. All I knew was that it was a big wooded area way out on the northwest side of town, where people went to have picnics. It was not until about 1930, when we moved to 706 N. 25th St., that the park became a reality to us, as it was only a few blocks west and within easy walking distance.

In 1930, when I was a Tilghman High School junior, I tried to get the job of manager of the football team. I learned that Curtis Sanders, the Tilghman football coach, was the man to see and I would have to go to Noble Park to talk to him, as his summertime job was as golf pro at the municipal golf course. At that time, the course was at Annie Baumer Field, adjoining the park. So I made a number of trips there during that summer, trying to get in with him. I didn't get the job as my classmate Jimmie Distler was his caddymaster and beat me out easily. At that age, golf was beyond the range of my pocketbook and it was some years later that I got hooked on golf, which I now play most weekdays, weather permitting.

Back in the 1930s, softball was all the rage. For quite a few seasons, there were leagues sponsored by local merchants and most boys of high school age and up became members of one of the teams. There was intense rivalry among all the teams and each year there was a tournament to determine the champion. These games drew huge crowds every night, with rooters pulling for their favorites. There were then and are still now, a number of diamonds sandwiched between the main park and the earthen flood wall. I was a member of the Ritz Ramblers, sponsored by the Ritz Hotel and the Dewey Payne Insurance Company. Our team was composed of some of the younger boys and was very popular when we beat better teams. One year we almost beat the perennial powerhouse, the Coca-Cola team, but lost by one run in the last of the ninth.

In 1937, a concrete swimming pool of 100 by 200 feet, was constructed by the Public Works Administration (WPA) on the west side of the park near the four tennis courts. A number of my friends were lifeguards there every summer. Our very fine swim team used the park to train and practice for meets that were held every summer. On the team with me were Burgess and Ed Scott, Euclid Covington, Luke Nichol, George Barkley, Gus Smith, Albert Otto and Allard Hardy.

When Park Avenue was widened, the stone wall along the street had to be torn down to provide width for the added lanes. The contractor was supposed to build the wall back, but somehow it was never done.

During the summer of 1988, Paducah Mayor Gerry Montgomery and McCracken County Judge Executive John Harris appointed a 16-member committee of city and county residents to study all the Paducah and county parks. There were over 360 acres in the city and 75 in the county. Because it was over 125 acres, Noble Park was given a high priority for any improvement. I served on that committee, along with other business and professional people. In June of 1990, a 10-year construction and renovation plan was proposed, estimated to cost $9 million to $10 million. It was not long until this plan was approved and today we have a beautiful park with many new features and facilities and with space available for future expansion.

Several years ago, it was determined that the original archway was deteriorating and needed to be replaced. We now have a new entrance and it closely resembles the old one. The original bronze tablets have been saved and are securely stored by the park board, with plans to have them replaced in an appropriate location in the near future.

In 1965, after the new city hall was built and the old one demolished, the city clock was removed and Mayor Tom Wilson had it stored at Noble Park, behind the residence of the park superintendent. It was mounted on a platform about six feet high and the clock was wrapped in a tarpaulin and securely tied with rope. After storage there for a few years, it disappeared.

Kolb family and Kolb Park

Originally, Broad Street was part of the acreage purchased by the Langstaff family, who moved here from New Jersey in the mid-1800s. They established the Langstaff-Orm Lumber Company along the banks of the Tennessee River. This was a workers' community named Jersey or Jerseyville, for the Langstaffs' former home state. Most residents worked at the lumber company or in one of the nearby 19th century factories.

In 1887, Louis Kolb, a German immigrant who operated a Paducah meat packing plant, bought the lot in the 1800 block of Broad Street from the Langstaff family and built a two-story brick house, which remains there today. One of the distinctive features of the old Kolb home is the octagon-shaped corner tower still visible from the street, despite the trees that surround the front and side of the lot. Kolb built a slaughter house in the back part of the lot, which was right on the bank of the Island Creek. The business remained there until the late 1940s. Today, more than 100 years later, there are still a few members of the Kolb family living on Broad Street.

In 1912, when there was a row of three Kolb residences on Broad Street, Louis Kolb sold a triangular plot of land along 6th and Broad to the City of Paducah for a city park. Because the sale price was considered unusually low, the city named the plot Kolb Park, in his honor. Kolb Park has been a good location for residents of the south side. Most of the growth of Paducah was on the north and west sides of the city, so Kolb Park has been given less attention than other larger parks. It has playground equipment and a nice swimming pool. In the hot summer months, it offers a place for youngsters to cool off and endure the weather.

One of Louis Kolb's daughters, Miss Rosa Kolb, was my Sunday School teacher for several years. My brother and I lived in the old Kolb home one summer in the 1920s while our parents were vacationing in Texas.

A son, Frank Kolb, in 1906, established the Kolb Drug Company, which became one of the largest wholesale drug distributors in western Kentucky. A grandson, Frank Kolb Jr., who lived in Mayfield, was a member of the local chapter of the Military Order of the Purple Heart. He served with the 1st Infantry Division in World War II and fought through Sicily and Africa. He was captured by the enemy in North Africa, but escaped to later storm the beaches of Normandy on D-Day and survive through the Battle of the Bulge. He earned four Silver Stars, a bronze star and the Purple Heart in seven campaigns. His cousin, Gus E. Hank, III, a member of the 78th Infantry Division in World War II, also earned the Purple Heart.

Wallace Park, George Wallace, Wallace House

Some may remember Wallace Park, located just beyond the intersection of 32nd and Broadway and embracing 75 acres. It was developed by the Paducah Traction Company, as our streetcar system was named, which in 1911, maintained 17 miles of track and more than 30 streetcars. The public was urged to "take the trolley to beautiful Wallace Park, an ideal pleasure resort where rest and recreation may be enjoyed and life-giving air inhaled." They boasted that the park could be reached by trolley from any part of the city for a five-cent fare. On a typical weekend, a single motor-car would haul up to 15 open trailer cars loaded with people. The use of the park declined in the 1920s. In 1922, Paducah made a great effort to obtain a western state teacher's college, offering the park as the site for the new college and campus. The award went to Murray and in 1925, the land was sold for residential development.

The one-story Wallace house was built by Philip Wallace around 1858 and is still in use today. It is owned by Julian Nichol, whose family for many years owned and operated the Paducah Lumber & Manufacturing Company on North 9th Street, the site of the old Cohankus Company.

Philip Wallace's son, George Wallace, lived in the house before becoming an adult. George Wallace founded the Wallace Vinegar Works in 1911. It was a flourishing business, which occupied the site which later became M. Livingston Wholesale Grocery Company. George married May Wisdom, daughter of one of Paducah's early millionaires, Benjamin Wisdom, whose old home at 914 Jefferson is on the National Register of Historic Places.

Around 1886, George Wallace built a new home on North 9th Street which later became famous as the Ninth Street House, owned by Curtis and Norma Grace. In the 1930s, the house was Martin's Boarding House where you could get a big meal for 35 cents.

Caldwell Park

One of the least known of the city parks is Caldwell Park. For many years there was a monument there, with a statue dedicated to the memory of Almyr Sherrell Edwards, who was a member of the Kentucky State Guard. He was shot and killed while on duty at the Guard Armory at 2nd and Jefferson the night of July 13, 1892, during a raid which resulted in the theft of several hundred rounds of ammunition and a few guns. There had been some racial tension for several weeks after a black man was hanged. The statue was vandalized and torn down about 1932 and only the base remains. Time has erased some of the inscription, but it is still legible.

This park, a triangular plot at Burnett, Park and 13th streets, was donated to the city by the heirs of Dr. Samuel B. Caldwell, a practicing physician from 1855 to 1870. In his later years, he spent most of his time and energies in real estate. Caldwell received his formal education in civil engineering. He put this knowledge to good use as he surveyed lots between Fountain Avenue and Arcadia and purchased the majority of property west of Fountain.

He became president of the West End Improvement Company in 1891. This company owned 116 acres on both sides of Broadway west of Fountain. He built several fine homes in the west end and provided the lots later purchased by former well-known businessmen, including Finis Lack, Robert Reeves and Oscar Hank, who built substantial homes in the 2800 block on Broadway. Dr. Caldwell also was president of the Lovelaceville Gravel & Road Company on West Broadway and a stockholder in the Electric Street Railway Company. As the street railway lines ran out to the Illinois Central passenger depot, many of the rails were on the street that is now called Caldwell.

People Famous
and
Interesting

Buck Willingham, the Cat and the Fiddle and the Twinkling Star

On Oct. 23, 1999, there was a notice in the *Paducah Sun* of the death of Marie Clark, 87, of Paducah, formerly Marie Robertson. Marie owned the Twinkling Star Restaurant at 3102 Broadway from 1934 to 1979. Since then, the ownership has changed many times. It was the Flamingo Restaurant at the time of her death.

This brings back many memories of that place. I remember when it was built in 1933 by Tom "Buck" Willingham, son of Dr. and Mrs. Willingham, who owned the property, which was adjacent to the doctor's home on the southeast corner of 32nd and Broadway. It was named the Cat and the Fiddle until acquired by Marie and her husband, Herman Jewel Robertson, and renamed the Twinkling Star. (Robertson, a chemistry teacher at Tilghman High married his former student Marie Mitchell, who graduated in 1929, in my sister's class).

It opened the same year I began working at Petter Supply. I did not own a car, but shared the family car with my brother Harry, until I earned enough to have one of my own. If it was his turn to use the car when a special event came up, I asked a friend to let me double date with him. After a dance or a show, we usually stopped at either "Jumbo" Thurman's Peacock Garden , located in the building now occupied by Dr. William Walden DDS, near 30th and Broadway, or at the Cat and the Fiddle. When the latter became the Twinkling Star, our visits were less frequent, as other night spots were being built and we had many more choices.

During the 1937 flood, water covered Paducah as far west as 29th Street and the Twinkling Star became Paducah City Hall, with "Command Headquarters" set up there.

I saw very little of Buck from the time he sold out until he and I were drafted into the Army. I was aware, though, of his activities with a number of business people around town. I later learned that Buck's partner at the Cat and the Fiddle was Dexter Howell, owner of the pool room in the basement of the Irvin Cobb Hotel and several businesses downtown.

Buck was a student at Tilghman High School and a member of the football team when I entered the school as a freshman in 1927. He starred in several games I attended in 1927 and 1928.

When he, George "Brownie" Wedel and I were drafted in October of 1942, we rode the bus together to Fort Benjamin Harrison, then rode the train to Jefferson Barracks in St. Louis, Mo., for basic training. On the train, Buck started a crap game. After showing Brownie and me a toothpaste package he had filled with loaded dice, we expected him to win. While we slept, Buck and other draftees shot craps into the night. When we asked Buck the next morning how he fared, he told us he lost most of his money, but was setting the others up and would win big the next time. That next time never came, for later that day, all the winners had shipped out.

About the fourth week of basic training, we were required to go through the obstacle course every day. It was pretty exhausting and many men were not in good physical condition and got through only with the greatest difficulty. After the first day that we went through, Buck told us he wasn't going to go through it again. He said he had an old football injury which enabled him to throw his shoulder out of joint easily. The next day, he was taken to the infirmary and went from there to the base hospital.

A few days later, we visited him in his ward. He said he was back to normal and had a doctor's certificate, which meant he wouldn't have to do the obstacle course. He said, "Look at that poor soldier in the bed next to me." He told us that when the guy was told he was slated to ship overseas, he went home on furlough that weekend and shot off his big toe. Every morning when his doctor came in, he looked at the man's chart and asked him, "Well, soldier, how is that toe today?" The man said, "Doc, it's still off." Buck had a highly-developed sense of humor and kept us in stitches with his sardonic assessment of all of us "sad sacks," who looked pretty ratty as we lined up every day. For me, his wit and humor made the first weeks of Army life bearable.

Several weeks later, I learned in a letter from home that Buck was a civilian again. He parlayed that certificate into an honorable discharge.

I saw Buck quite frequently after my return to civilian life, mostly in the evenings when I would run into him at Rolling Hills Country Club, where he was on the board of directors. Or I saw him at one of the Army veteran's clubs.

He died in 1986 at the age of 77. I knew his sisters, Estelle, who married my dentist, Dr. Glenn Donoho, a close friend and hunting partner of Stanley Petter, and the younger sister, Euleene Willingham, who was as witty and full of fun as Buck.

Paul Twitchell

The name Paul Twitchell is well known to many. His biography and genealogy are well documented in the files of the Paducah Public Library. There is information about his growing up in Paducah, attending local public schools, working at the YMCA and serving as trainer and assistant coach for the basketball and football teams at Augusta Tilghman High School. Also, there is data about his working at the Paducah Marine Ways on the river front, where his father, Jacob, and brother, Howard, worked for years. His sister, Katherine, worked in the music department at Wilson's Book Store most of her adult life.

Paul was a student at Murray State and served as a trainer and coach's assistant for basketball and football. The Paducah directories listed him as a painter at the Marine Ways and later, as a clerk for Gulf Oil. The 1941 city directory listed him as a self-employed writer. His resume was listed in the 1939 edition of "Who's Who in Kentucky," and said he had completed 20 years in physical education in two colleges and at two small YMCAs.

He enlisted in the Navy in 1942, was soon commissioned an ensign, was promoted to full lieutenant and was up for lieutenant commander when he was discharged shortly before V-E Day September, 1945. While in the Navy, he married Camille Ballowe, a Paducah native. He became a correspondent for "Our Navy" and was assigned to Washington, D.C.

During their time in the East, Paul and Camille attended many religious services. They joined the Self Revelation Church of Absolute Monism, founded by an East Indian leader, who would profoundly influence Paul's spiritual life. Their association continued for eight years.

It was then that there were many changes in Paul's life. He and Camille were divorced and Paul moved out west. He became a rebel in society and referred to this period as his "cliffhanger" days. He drove a small sports car, wearing an assortment of strange sports caps and drank only champagne. He was a frequent patron of the Seattle, Washington, library and became a prodigious reader, carrying off books by the armload. He met and married a Washington College student who worked at the library.

A transition occurred then from "cliffhanger" to spiritual leader of a religious order named "Eckankar," an Eastern religion based on "The Ancient Science of Soul Travel." He became a "Living Eckmaster" in 1965 and began writing discourses for his new followers. In less than three years, he attracted followers said to number more than 300,000. In the space of six years, Paul published 26 books. It is said he received from 6,000 to 10,000 letters a week.

Paul began giving talks all over the country. On Sept. 16, 1971, he arrived in Cincinnati to appear at an Eck seminar, but was found dead in his room the next day. An article in a 1982 issue of the *Courier-Journal* referred to his life as a "Strange odyssey, a multi-million dollar religious cult which stands as a reminder of the mysterious and checkered existence of Paul Twitchell."

Recollections of Paul Twitchell

My first remembrance of Paul Twitchell was in the 1920s at the YMCA, when it was at 709 Broadway. We began to frequent the "Y" after school and on weekends and Paul was our swim instructor and coach for basketball and volleyball. A large number of boys my age belonged to the Y and participated in team sports. We had certain hours when we could use the facilities, and though it was a young men's organization, girls could use the pool and gym during certain hours.

During the early 1930s, Paul organized a swimming team among some of the better swimmers. Those who made the team were Euclid Covington; Gus Smith; Otto Clark; Luke Nichol; Burgess, Ed and Joe Scott; Oscar McCutcheon and me. My assignment was the backstroke, breaststroke and being alternate man on the four-man freestyle relay. Otto, one of the older swimmers, was a veteran diver.

Paul coached the basketball teams which played intra-squad games at night. He was not a talented athlete himself, but was an excellent coach, knew the rules and how to teach the fundamentals. He was small in stature, about five-foot-six, with a chunky well-muscled body and bowed legs.

Paul was in my grade at Tilghman High School, but I don't think he ever graduated and was not present for the ceremony. He was not listed in any of the class albums from 1929 through 1932, a year after I graduated. We considered him a class member, though, in our 1931 class album. In the class prophecy written by Burgess Scott, Paul was mentioned as a hobo at the 28th reunion. An artist drawing showed a bowlegged, bewhiskered man at a campfire.

Although I don't remember Paul being in any of my classes

except physical education, he was a trainer and assistant to football and basketball Coach Curtis Sanders during my last two high school years. He helped the football line coach with offense and defense strategies, worked with the kickers and taught dribbling and guarding to the basketball team members.

I was on the 1930-1931 track teams and ran the 100-yard dashes and relays. It was the only sport for which I received a letter. There at every practice session was Paul, assistant to our track Coach John M. Logsdon, our journalism teacher who had been a trackman at the University of Chicago. Paul was also the trainer and saw to it that we ran our laps around the track and took our wind sprints. Our final year was our best, as we won most meets. We took first place at the Murray regionals and won the Kentucky state championship at Bowling Green.

As a result, we were invited to take runners to the National Interscholastic Track Meet to be held that year at the University of Chicago. Our team could only take the few runners with the most

Paul Twitchell

points. Paul drove to Chicago with us. We took two cars, as there were eight of us. At that time, gas was very cheap; at most places along the way we paid 15 cents a gallon. There were a few track-side stations that offered "white gas" at nine cents, which we used every chance we got. We didn't have to pay our way, but were told the budget for the trip was limited.

It took all day to get there. We registered at the field office in the stadium and were assigned quarters in one of the fraternity houses near the field. We were put in one room on the second floor, where space had been cleared and folding cots were placed for us to use. Our top sprinter, George Barkley, nephew of Senator Alben Barkley, and I were the last to enter the room and saw that all the cots were chosen, except for one by the front window overlooking the campus and one way back in a dark corner. George and I both dashed for the one by the window and fell on it to claim possession. The force broke off one leg and split the canvas. Paul, who had a room upstairs with the other coaches, heard the commotion and

Paul Twitchell

came to our room to see what was happening. Since we both claimed to have gotten there first, Paul told me I had to sleep in the broken cot, as George was our best man and had the best chance of winning and deserved to sleep where he could get a good night's rest.

I said I would not sleep there and would sit up all night in the wooden chair nearby. I was told I was stubborn, selfish, uncooperative and to just be stubborn and stay in the chair. Paul stormed out of the room and stomped up the stairs to his room. I sat there for an hour reading a magazine. After a while, when all was quiet and I assumed everyone was asleep, I thought I might as well try the cot and get what sleep I could. About that time I heard footsteps. I saw the door slowly open and Paul peek in. He walked over to the chair, muttered how stubborn I was and left. I sat there until I heard the upstairs door close, then climbed into the broken cot and slept as best I could. I woke up a lot, as it was not comfortable. I woke up early and went back to the chair and began reading. I had not been there over a few minutes, when Paul came to check on me. When he saw me in the chair and assumed I had been there all night, he stood looking at me for a moment. Then all he said was, "Damn," and turned around and left.

At the stadium, we saw athletes from all over the country. Spectators trickled in and by the time the meet started the stadium was pretty full. In every event, ribbons and medals were awarded to the first six places. As we watched the early races, we could tell we were competing against the nation's top runners and that we would have to extend ourselves to even score. Our top sprinters were nowhere near the winners. The last race was our four-man relay, with each man running a 110-yard leg. We lined up against 11 other teams and managed to come in sixth. It was our only win. We each received a ribbon and small bronze medal, with the team getting the sixth place medal. I still have these in a frame in my den.

On the way home, we each told how much we enjoyed the experience and were happy to see the top athletes and that we were happy to have at least scored. Paul was riding with us and turned to me and said, "You know, if you had not been so stubborn and gotten a full night's rest, who knows, we might have been able to make a better showing."

Captain Louis H. Igert

Captain Louis H. Igert, founder of the Igert Towing Company, was born in Leavenworth, Ind. He was the son of a common laborer and had to quit school after the fourth grade, when his father died. In later years, he said his first

Irvin Cobb and Captain Louis Igert

enterprise as a boy of nine was hauling passengers across high Ohio River backwater on a raft of butternut logs at his father's farm. When he was 15, he worked at a spoke factory in Leavenworth. He worked a 10-hour shift six days a week and took home a weekly wage of $1.50. Every other Sunday, he helped load spokes onto a steamboat for 20 cents an hour. After the spoke factory was shut down, he got a job as a deck hand, traveling the Ohio and Mississippi rivers for $1 a day.

Around 1900, he worked for a company that was dredging mussel shell for buttons. He worked his way up to a position of responsibility and began managing button factories along the river, occasionally operating as an independent. In the meantime, he

Towboat Irvin S. Cobb with Cobb and Louis Igert on Deck

operated a sideline business hauling railroad ties and other com-
modities. He came to Paducah in 1917 as an employee of the
branch factory of McKee Button of Muscatine, Iowa. During the off
seasons he operated boats on the Ohio and Tennessee.

He organized his own company in 1927 and at its peak,
operated 12 boats and 80 barges. Among those he owned were the
Louis Igert; Emmy, named for Mrs. Igert; Philip Ritchie, named for
a partner; Clarendon; Paducah; Bedford; Vixen; Florita; Stanley
Petter; and Irvin S. Cobb. I have pictures of these nine boats which
were generously given to me by a long-time friend and part owner,
W.W. "Bill" Dyer, who married Julia Igert.

Capt. Igert was active in many civic functions, was one of
the original members of the Selective Service Board, helped the
Business and Professional Women's Club acquire a clubhouse and
made contributions to the Aldersgate Methodist Church in its early
days.

During the flood of 1937, his company operated four barges
in flood relief, carrying and sheltering refugees. He bought out the
stock of two groceries to feed those in need and opened his home at
320 N. 7th St., providing coffee and doughnuts for relief workers
and doctors. He bought a carload of chickens from the Illinois
Central Railroad and estimated he furnished 15,000 meals during
the flood. He belonged to the Elks Club, Masonic Lodge 449 of
Paducah Mizpah, Shrine Temple and was a member of the Broadway
Methodist Church. He died in 1963 at the age of 79.

Captain Igert
and the McKee Button Company

I became acquainted with Captain Louis Igert when I began work in the early 1930s at the Petter Supply Company. Besides being a good customer, Igert was a long-time friend of Stanley Petter. The captain would occasionally stop in the Petter office to visit while there to purchase supplies for his fleet of tugboats. Since Petter catered to the river industry, the company stocked many items used regularly, such as manila and wire rope, towing ratchets, chain and oakum and caulking cotton (for wooden barges). Also stocked were items especially required by mussel fishermen, such as seine twine and annealed wire for making mussel hooks.

At his peak, Igert would bankroll a number of small mussel fishermen, supplying them with twine, hooks, pipe for racks and even boats, if necessary.

Igert left the McKee Button Company in 1927, when his independent towing business required his full-time attention. McKee hired A.L. Miller to operate the button factory. He stayed until 1934, when H.E. Castleman replaced him. In 1937, Albert S. McKee of Muscatine, Iowa, closed the plant, but continued to buy mussel shells from local fishermen and had them shipped to Muscatine.

During the last four years of operation in Paducah, I made a number of deliveries to the plant, which was located on the Tennessee River bank at 1310 S. 3rd, just past the old Shelton-Hougland Precision Machine Shop. Next to it were several large storage oil tanks, which are still there. The McKee plant had about 20 employees, most of them women. They wore heavy leather aprons, cotton gloves and rubber boots or heavy shoes. They stood at long benches with buckets of mussel shells nearby. They would empty a bucket of shells onto the bench, pry the shells open with curved knives, scoop out the meat into waste cans, separate the shell halves, then fill a bucket with shells which would be taken to the drill operators for cutting out the buttons. An experienced driller could get about eight buttons from the average size shell.

The work was hard. The women's hands were frequently cut by the sharp edges of shell and they used several pairs of gloves every day. The floors were always an inch or two deep in water. The odor was terrible, with a fishy smell always prevalent. After packing the buttons into large cartons for shipping, the shell remnants were shoveled into barrels and sold for fill. Many a driveway in Paducah was filled with these pieces which when crushed made a good solid drive.

Con Wilford Craig

When I lived on Harahan Boulevard in 1930, I became aware of Con Wilford Craig, who lived on Jefferson Street, two blocks from our house. Con was very active with the Boy Scouts and was one of the men who each year helped Scout Executive Roy Manchester transport the Scouts to and from Camp Pakentuck, Ill. His son, Clark, was a Scout my age and on the Tilghman High School track team with me.

Con was also active in other civic affairs and served for several decades as executive secretary of the Paducah Board of Trade. At the time, he also was state highway commissioner for 42 western Kentucky counties.

Con was born in 1876 in Unionville, Ill., where his family owned a farm. He was 12 years old when his father died from injuries suffered in an accident in his wheat field. He left a struggling family of four on a mortgaged farm. Con was forced to quit school to help support the family, but worked on the farm in the day and kept up with school assignments at night. He entered high school in Metropolis, Ill., when his brother Joe was old enough to handle the farm work. To pay his way, he began working for A.H. Quarles, a grocer. At night he cleaned the law office of J.F. McCarthey, who permitted him to "read the law," which was the only way then to qualify to practice law. At age 18, he took a law quiz from Judge A.K. Vickers in Vienna, Ill., and passed.

Con went to west Texas and became a cowboy on the Goodnight Ranch near Amarillo. After driving cattle for over a year, he got homesick and decided to head home. He bought a little buckskin pony and rode it all the way from Texas to Unionville, a trip that took two weeks. He came to Paducah around 1900 and went to work for the J.E. Dickson Wholesale Grain Company on South 6th Street, where the Nashville, Chattanooga & St. Louis Railroad (NC&St.L) headquarters was situated later. The grain job lasted three years. Then Con got a job with the NC&St.L, and after a few years there became one of the top freight rate experts in the country.

For no good reason, he quit the railroad one day and got a job selling patent medicine and began traveling a large area out west. While going around, Con saw that some cities were growing and others shrinking, with people leaving slow-moving towns and going to those that had good spirit and drive. His thoughts dwelled on Paducah on the bank of the Ohio River with a handful of industrial plants, so he came back to Kentucky and in 1913 became the executive secretary of the board of trade.

The Illinois Central Railroad (ICRR) had been paying high rates for the old charter line which ran through Cairo, Ill., and wanted to build the Edgewood Cutoff, a straight line from Bluford, Ill., to Paducah. They could not get the approval of the Interstate Commerce Commission, so they asked Con for help. In 1923, this was approved and the ICRR was given this permit. Not long after, a grateful ICRR President Charles H. Markham came to Paducah in his private railroad car, conferred with Con and others and announced that the railroad had decided to build its $8 million shops here, instead of in Fulton, Ky., as originally planned.

After Prohibition ended the distillery business in Paducah and the large building which housed the Friedman-Keiler Distillery Company at 2nd and Jefferson became empty, George Goodman, president of the board of trade asked Con to contact the International Shoe Company in St. Louis and try to get them to buy the plant. After 31 trips by Con to see Frank Rand, the shoe company president, Rand set in motion the project which brought the

Board of Trade President, Con W. Craig

plant and 700 jobs to Paducah.

Other industries which came here as a result of Con's effort were the Magnavox plant on North 8th Street; the Walter T. Kelley beehive factory in Lone Oak; Bowes Industries, makers of paper plates; Deena Artware on South 3rd; Normandy Frocks; and the M. Fine & Sons shirt factory on North 8th.

Con assisted with the organization of the McCracken County Strawberry Association, a co-op which helped Paducah become known as the strawberry capitol of the world.

While waiting in Brookport for the ferry to resume operations after being shut down due to high winds, Con realized the great impact a bridge would have on both Kentucky and Illinois. He contacted Rep. Alben Barkley, seeking his help. That required the issuance of $1,256,000 in bridge bonds, and in 1929, the new bridge was opened to traffic, saving regular users countless hours of driving.

Con Craig was a member of the Rotary Club of Paducah and of Broadway Methodist Church. His daughter, Nell, married George Hughes, a long-time employee of the People's National Bank and was there the few years my wife, Zelma, worked there before we married. Con died in 1958 at the age of 81.

Herbie Tade

This is the story of Herbert S. Tade, a young man who at age 20 was injured in a college football game and was an invalid for the remaining 35 years of his life. "Herbie," as he was known all his life, attended Washington Junior High School and began his athletic career under the tutelage of Otis Dinning, who saw in Herbie a natural athlete with the promise of becoming a top-notch basketball and football player. Whenever Coach Dinning began practice basketball sessions in the old junior high gym on the third floor, his call-out was always Herbie first, then the rest of the players.

As soon as he was enrolled in Tilghman High School, Herbie went out for both basketball and football and became an All-State and All-Southern football back. After graduation, he went to the University of Tennessee at Knoxville and was their varsity center. Although he suffered a broken arm, crushed shoulder, broken feet and a bad knee, his desire to play was so strong that his courage overshadowed his physical defects. He was the mainstay of the team. While other players spent time on the bench resting, he played every minute.

Herbie was slated to become captain of the team in 1936, his senior year. Tall, nearly 21 and weighing 185 pounds, he had grown from a slender lad of 120 pounds when he entered high school.

His last game was the annual Thanksgiving Day Kentucky-Tennessee clash, a rivalry that existed for many years. More than 15,000 shivering fans witnessed the contest. Kentucky's Wildcats ran wild on a very muddy sod at Stoll Field at Lexington, winning 27-0. It was the first Kentucky victory over Tennessee since 1925. A charging drive through the center of the line by a trio of Kentucky backs was stopped by Tade on the one-yard line in the fourth quarter. But his defense was costly. Herbie was injured on the play and was carried from the field by his teammates and taken to Good Samaritan Hospital. His skull was fractured above the eye and there was little hope he would survive the night. A brain specialist performed a delicate operation to save his life. Afterwards, he never spoke or walked again and spent the rest of his life in a wheelchair, gallantly trying to communicate with family and friends in sign language. He remained an avid football fan and never missed a Tennessee game on radio and television. The university sent him a season pass for home games every year.

In 1959, special arrangements were made for Tade to attend a Tennessee-Mississippi game at Knoxville. His brother Bill and Dr. W.H. England of Lone Oak took him to Knoxville, where he was escorted to the stadium by police, welcomed by Coach Bowden Wyatt and recognized by the cheerleaders.

When told about Herbie's injury, Tilghman High School Principal Walter C. Jetton said, "Of all the boys we turned out at Tilghman, Herbie was the best equipped to take advantage of a college education and to play football. We have never produced a finer youngster or one with higher ideals."

Colonel Augustus S. Thompson

In the late 1920s, my father moved his grocery from 621 Broadway to Broadway near 10th Street. We soon became acquainted with the Thompson Transfer Company in the next block at 1015 Broadway. Thompson employees not only became frequent customers of ours, but were the truck drivers who brought freight to us daily from the Illinois Central and Nashville-Chattanooga & St. Louis depots.

Col. Gus Thompson was the owner and Miss Bess Gockel was general manager. They still used horses and wagons to deliver freight to all the merchants in town. Several of the teams pulled large wagons which required pairs of large draft horses. All the drivers were black men, most of whom had been in Thompson's employ for many years. Some were quite elderly. Most walked to Dad's store around noon and bought food for their lunches. One driver was Lum, a large muscular man who seemed to be able to handle the heavy loads with ease.

Our store policy was "cash and carry," and we had no system for credit accounts. At first, a few of Thompson's men asked us to "hold the ticket" until the weekend. Since the men were daily customers and the amounts were small, we did this for a few. But after a while, the occasions became more frequent and we soon found it was getting out of hand.

Dad told me to go talk to Thompson or Miss Gockel, collect what was owed and tell them we would have to have the men pay cash in the future. Although the men told us they were paid each weekend, we learned they were paid in cash at noon each day. Apparently, Thompson learned the pattern of his employees and knew that if they were paid once a week, they would spend it all over the weekend and be broke by Monday. His policy of paying in cash each noonday proved to be a way to keep them on the job all day every day. Miss Gockel said she would not be responsible for their debts and would not withhold what they owed us. Dad charged off their indebtedness to bad judgment.

Col. Thompson, a bachelor, lived upstairs over the business. He was well known and respected and also known around the United States as a horseman's horseman and considered the best judge of horses in the country. For almost 50 years, he officiated at the biggest horse shows in the United States. His judging engagements included shows in Madison Square Garden, Kansas City, Louisville, Lexington, St. Louis, the San Francisco World's Fair and Toronto, Canada.

He owned a number of trotters and pacers and was an active participant during the summer harness racing season. He loved to show saddle horses, particularly his favorite mounts, Brilliant Miss and Bourbon Annabelle. His harness horses were George Goodman,

Dick Lumpkin, Cedar Lake Girl and Posey Potemkin. He seldom missed a day of working or watching his horses at Carson Park.

A Paducah native, Thompson was the son of Dr. Joseph W. Thompson, an Illinois Central chief surgeon, and Victoria O'Brien. He was manager of the Paducah Railway Company in the days of mule-drawn streetcars. His partners in the transfer company were Sam Hubbard and W.B. Kennedy, both of whom he bought out after two years. At the time, he had about 150 head of horses and mules. In the latter years, he added motorized trucks.

He loved to entertain horse lovers from all over the country in his apartment, which was furnished with horse motif. All the furniture coverings were decorated with horse prints of various kinds and he had lamps, ash trays, bookends and dozens of pieces with spurs, horseshoes and bits. On the walls were show ribbons and pictures of horses and horsemen.

In 1947, while participating in a race at the West Kentucky Fair, he was thrown from his sulky and suffered a broken shoulder bone and fractured nose. Although it was predicted he would never ride again, he was back at it a few months later. But a year later, he fell at his office and suffered a broken hip, which ended his racing career. He had to abandon the upstairs apartment and took a room on Jefferson Street in the home of Miss Gockel, who had managed the transfer business for more than 40 years. A week before he died, he drove to Carson Park to watch his trotter, Gus Thompson, in workouts. He was admitted to the Illinois Central Hospital on a Saturday after suffering a heart attack and died quietly in his sleep early the next day. He refused to divulge his age and when asked, replied, "I'm smooth-mouthed, but I'm sound."

Captain Robert Hunter Noble

*I*t is doubtful that anyone living in Paducah or the surrounding area would not know Noble Park. Most residents have either been there or driven by the ornamental archway that graces its entrance, or at least, know where it is. Most know the park was named for Bob Noble, who donated money to purchase the land.

But I doubt if very many people, including long-time residents, know very much about the man who left such a visible landmark for Paducah. Bob Noble was the son of Colonel John C. Noble and Elizabeth Pierson Noble. His father, a colonel in the Confederate Army, was a publisher and printer and operated a newspaper in Louisville when Bob was born in 1855. The family moved to Paducah when Bob was two years old and Col. Noble established a newspaper called the *Paducah Herald.* A morning paper, it enjoyed a wide circulation for many years. Bob attended Paducah schools and also was a pupil in the Catholic school operated by priests.

On moving to Paducah, Col. Noble built a house at the intersection of the Lone Oak and Blandville roads, which later became known as Cedar Lake, and for many years was the home of Mr. and Mrs. Ed D. Hannan. At present, it is the location of Hannan Plaza.

As a young adult, Bob traveled for his brother, Ed P. Noble, who operated a wholesale grocery firm. Later he was engaged in the transfer business. In 1913, he established the Ohio Valley Sand & Gravel Company, merging several small sand digging companies into what was to become one of the largest industries of its kind in the South. In 1928, Noble sold the business to a group of industrialists, and it became known as the Federal Materials Company when its president, Norman Hely, moved here from Cape Girardeau to operate the business.

Capt. Noble was a member of the Paducah Park Board of Commissioners for many years and took an active interest in the development of the city's park system and playgrounds. Richard Rudy, for many years president of the Citizen's Bank, served with Noble on the park board. Capt. Noble made a gift of $10,000 to the city for the purchase of the 110-acre tract of wooded unimproved land, which was converted into the beautiful park which bears his name. He loved the park and frequently visited it, even after his health began to fail.

Although not a member of any church, he was a man of charitable nature and took pleasure in contributing to the city's religious advancement. He made a number of substantial gifts to Grace Episcopal Church, where his parents and family members were affiliated. Through the rector, the Rev. Custis Fletcher, Capt. Noble made many gifts to deserving black churches in the city. Noble often told his friends that while in the transfer business, he employed many black laborers and learned to appreciate their industry and loyalty.

Capt. Noble lived for a number of years at 2007 Jefferson St. He never married. He is buried in the family plot in Oak Grove Cemetery. When the entrance to Noble Park was built, a bronze tablet was erected in honor of Capt. Noble. Carved on the tablet was a tribute written by Irvin S. Cobb, who called him a "true southern gentleman."

John Marvin Steele

rivate John Marvin Steele, a paratrooper of the 2nd Battalion 505th Regiment of the 82nd Airborne Division, a veteran of jumps in Sicily and Italy during World War II, sat in the dark loaded plane, ready for the D-Day invasion across the English Channel to open a second front and shorten the war with Germany. Eight hundred and eighty-two planes droned through the early morning hours, dropping 13,000 paratroopers of the 82nd and 101st airborne divisions in the field behind the German defenses along the Normandy coast.

John Steele's 'chute opened perfectly and he floated down through the darkness of the night, but something went wrong. Instead of the pre-arranged drop zone, he was heading for the center of a French village. The place was on fire and German soldiers were frantically running about. As it seemed to Steele, they were all looking up at him. A bullet smashed into his foot, but worse than that, he was heading straight for the church steeple. The 'chute caught on the spire and he dangled helplessly. He was an inviting target. He tried to cut himself loose, but his knife slipped out of his hand and fell onto the pavement below, which drew a burst of gunfire. He decided quickly to play dead and for two hours as he dangled to and fro, he simulated death. He said he was helpless and scared.

The Germans eventually cut him down to strip him of his rations and found that he was still alive. They took him prisoner, but several days later he escaped during an American tank attack and made it back to friendly lines. Later in December, after two weeks in an English hospital, he dropped into Holland and was among those who helped drive through to beleaguered Bastogne, where the 101st was surrounded in the "Battle of the Bulge."

This story has been recounted in the book, *The Longest Day*, by Cornelius Ryan and in a movie of the same name with Red

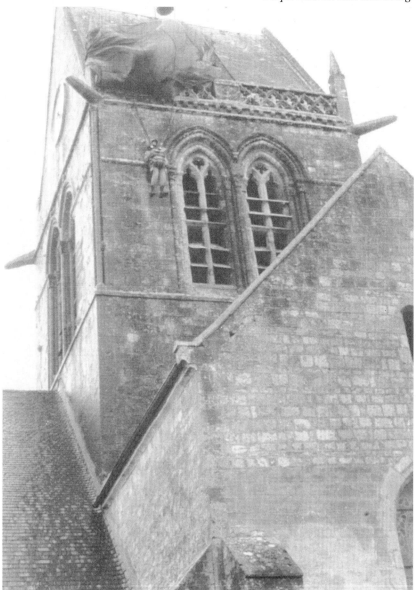

Sgt. John Steele, Metropolis Native, on Steeple of church at St. Mere Eglise, France, D-Day, June 6, 1944

Buttons playing the part of John Steele. Norman "Short Dog" Steele, one of John's brothers, was killed in Germany on April 16, 1945, just three weeks before the end of World War II in Europe.

John Marvin Steele was the son of Capt. John Henry and Josephine Lynn Steele of Metropolis, Ill.. Capt. Steele was a riverboat pilot for many years and was elected sheriff for a four-year term in 1938.

One of John's sisters, Mary Elizabeth, married John R. Harris, who saw service in the Navy and later became judge executive of the McCracken County Court.

(This transcribed from the Massac County Historical Society book in the Paducah Public Library.)

Jack Staulcup

During the Big Band Era of the 1930s and 1940s, the two most popular local bands were those of Jack Staulcup and Harry Ware. This is the story of Jack Staulcup, who lived in Metropolis, but was so often booked in Paducah many thought he lived here.

Jack was born in Martin, Tenn., in 1907 and was graduated from Grove High School in Paris, Tenn. He formed a three-piece combo in Paris and played in the pit of the Capitol Theater for silent motion pictures. He played the saxophone and clarinet and he sang. A girl named Juanita played piano and another friend played the drums. Jack wrote his own theme song, "Nita," and named it after Juanita. Each musician made $30 a week, playing six nights a week at the theater. As that was back in the 1920s, it was considered good pay.

After high school, Jack joined the Frank Silca Orchestra, a traveling dance band, and later joined the Dixie Melody Boys, who were located in Metropolis. In 1927, Jack moved to Metropolis, started dating Ethel Moreland and married her in 1930. They had two boys, Jack Jr., and Brent Lee. He stayed with the Dixie Melody Boys until 1932, when he started his own band

Because he played here so often, many Paducahans were not aware of his reputation elsewhere. He received rave reviews in dozens of towns throughout the South, where he played to packed houses. My first memory of Staulcup was when he would sit-in with

Jack Staulcup

Harry Ware's orchestra, while playing engagements at the Irvin Cobb Hotel. He had just formed his own band and arranged with the Cobb manager to play in the dining room and in the ballroom for dancing on Saturday nights. Later on, he was booked during the summer months for dances held on the roof of the Cobb. Meanwhile, he was booking dance engagements all over the South, Midwest and in a few cities in the East.

This started his career as a traveling dance band. He played at the Roseland Ballroom in New York City, Brighton Beach in New Jersey, Vanity Ballroom in Detroit and at the Commodore Perry Hotel in Toledo. At first, he had several booking agents, but as his popularity increased, he decided he could do his own booking.

Jack dearly loved music and never considered being anything but a musician. He had a heart attack in 1973, was in Western Baptist Hospital for five weeks, but went back with his band after six weeks of convalescence. He had a second heart attack in 1981, but was back with the band again in a few weeks. He became ill again in 1984 and was in and out of the hospital until he died in May, 1985. His last wish was, "Please don't let my band go down the drain. It was the best band I ever had." So his widow leased the band to Bill French of Cape Girardeau, who kept it going for a while, until big bands slowly faded from the scene.

Vernon Carver Rudolph

ernon Carver Rudolph was born on a farm in Marshall County, came to Paducah after high school, started peddling doughnuts door-to-door and in a few years built his Krispy-Kreme Doughnut Company into a nationwide chain.

Vernon was born in 1915, the eldest of five children. His parents, Plumie Harrison and Rethie Rudolph, owned a farm and small general store in the Haitt community. Vernon attended elementary school in Haitt and high school in Aurora, six miles away.

After graduating in 1933, he came to Paducah to work for his uncle Ishmael Armstrong, who operated a small neighborhood grocery on Hill Street. Armstrong sold his grocery and bought a doughnut shop on Broad Street from Joseph LeBeouf of Lake Charles, La., who had moved to Paducah to work for the Army Corps of Engineers. The purchase included not only the shop and all equipment, but the secret formula for the Krispy-Kreme doughnut. Vernon began selling and making deliveries from his bicycle.

They moved their business to Nashville as the demand for their doughnuts grew, and other family members joined the company. Back in Kentucky, Vernon's father, Plumie, closed his general store and went to work for the Nashville store. Within a few years, stores were opened in several other southern states.

In 1937, Vernon sold his interest in the Nashville store and moved to Winston-Salem, N.C., and with $200 rented a building across from Salem College on Main Street and opened his doughnut shop. The company prospered and expanded and in a few years became the corporate headquarters for a chain of doughnut shops in many large cities in the Southeast. The company operated a fleet of trucks to supply ingredients to all locations and built large bins and warehouses to hold the many tons of flour and other components of the doughnuts. Vernon died in 1973, was survived by his wife,

Lorrain, three sons and two daughters. His son, Vernon Carver Jr., is a realtor in Winston-Salem and has written most of the history of the company. His uncle, Lewis, a former vice president of the company, is retired and living in Nashville. Parents, grandparents and many Rudolph kin are buried in the Union Baptist Cemetery in the Haitt community in Marshall County.

Vernon Carver Rudolph

Joseph Gibbs LeBeouf

This story is about a Frenchman from Louisiana who moved to Paducah and worked for the Army Corps of Engineers until the corps shut down its Paducah operation. The story goes that in the 1930s, Joseph LeBeouf had a doughnut shop on Broad Street which he sold to Ishmael Armstrong, along with his secret doughnut formula. This formula was responsible for the birth of the Krispy-Kreme Doughnut Company. According to LeBeouf's daughter, Anna Dean, he never knew of the huge business that grew out of his formula.

Anna has supplied the following background and update about her father.

"He was born in Lake Charles, La., the eighth child of a family of 13. When he was 16 years old, his older brother who worked on the dredge boat the U.S. Lake Charles, came home and took him back to Texas and got him a job on the boat as cook/deck hand. This was the beginning of a 41-year career with the Army Corps of Engineers.

"In 1930, the government transferred him to Paducah. Shortly after this, he returned to Louisiana to marry my mother, Irma LeBlanc, and brought her back to Paducah. I was born in Paducah in 1933 and my sister, Barbara Sue, was born in 1936. Judy Adeline, our third sister, was born in 1945. Dad was then transferred to Louisville in 1949. Our youngest sister, Joan Marie, was born in Louisville in 1961.

"After he retired from the government, the City of Louisville bought the Belle of Louisville. The city hired several retired corps men to get the Belle up and running. Dad was the first mate for seven years. He actually hired the present Capt. Mike Fitzgerald when he was a youngster.

"Dad lived a full life and was 93 years old when he passed

away. He was never aware of the Krispy-Kreme Doughnut business. I know that he would have said something if he had. He never mentioned Ishmael Armstrong."

Joseph G. Lebeouf, First Mate, Belle of Louisville

The Goulds and Palmers

When Augusta Tilghman High School was built, a house on the property was left standing and was used for home economics classes and for a while, as a cafeteria. It later was demolished to make way for an addition, which was used for years as a symphony hall. This house, once at the address of 1014 Clark St., was owned by the Gould family and called The Ferns. Prior to being purchased by Sidell and Frederick Boyd Tilghman, it was the residence of Miss Fannie Gould and her sister, Mary Gould Palmer, widow of Elbridge Palmer, for whom the Palmer House Hotel is named.

The Tilghmans were the sons of General Lloyd Tilghman, a Confederate general, killed in the Battle of Vicksburg during the Civil War. His sons, though no longer living here, had fond memories of Paducah and to honor the family name, bought the Gould property for a new high school, which was named for their mother, Augusta Tilghman. The school was built and opened in 1921.

After selling their Clark Street home, Mary Palmer and Fannie Gould lived at 739 Broadway until 1935. Mrs. Palmer died in 1948 in New York and was brought back home and buried in the Gould family plot in Oak Grove Cemetery. Her sister, Frances, called, Fannie, died in 1955 and is also buried in the family plot.

Mary's husband, Elbridge, apparently was prominent in his day and an interesting man, though there is only sketchy information about him. He was born in 1833 and died at age 63. He was president of the City National Bank and is known for having pledged the money needed to construct the hotel, provided it was named for him, as it was.

Palmer also was president of the Paducah Furniture Manufacturing Company, which was incorporated in 1870. Charles H. Rieke was general manager. Company offices and salesroom were at 114-116 South St., with the factory on South 3rd between Tennessee and Norton. In 1895, Ed Woolfolk was made manager. The company employed about 100 people and kept four salesmen in the field.

A plaque honoring Elbridge Palmer occupies a prominent spot in the historical room of the Paducah Public Library. It was donated by Isaac Bernheim, who in 1933 paid for the addition to the library as a tribute to Palmer. Bernheim, an immigrant from Germany, was befriended by Palmer, who loaned him money without collateral, to start his own business.

The Sternwheeler Stanley Petter

The *Stanley Petter* was a small paddle boat built by the Igert Towing Company and named for Capt. Igert's good friend, Stanley Petter. This boat served for a number of years as part of the Igert fleet of 12 boats which formerly plied the Tennessee and Ohio rivers out of their home port, Paducah. It was a member of the cast of the movie, "How the West was Won," a part of which was filmed on the Ohio River at Smithland.

This boat was built in 1927 and hauled railroad ties, mussel shells and coal on the rivers for years. It wasn't much to look at, but an MGM talent scout for the movie thought its old battered countenance could be fixed up. He was able to convince the owners and invested $4,500 in the project. They added "gingerbread," two smokestacks, a swing stage, a "proud new look" and gave it three roles in the movie. After the filming was finished and the cast moved on to the next location, the *Stanley Petter* lay idle on the Tennessee River, so MGM gave orders to sell it.

At about the same time, in Chicago, Paul Buhl, executive of the Benson Fish Company and Allen LeClair, a licensed excursion boat captain and cultural arts chairman of the Congress of Parents and Teachers, were interested in locating a sternwheeler to start an excursion business. When Buhl learned the *Stanley Petter* was for sale, he and LeClair flew to Paducah, bought the boat and wondered how they could get it to Chicago.

That is when their troubles began. They decided to take it up river themselves. LeClair recruited Herbert Brusso, a mechanic, as chief engineer; Elmer Knize, a United Dye models designer, as first mate; and his wife, Jeanette as cook. All were expert sailors and all owned boats on Lake Michigan. They planned a three-week trip. It took nine.

The *Petter*, long idle in the hot, quiet river, had been supported between two barges and its seams were open. When they got it underway under its own power, water poured in, the electric pump cracked, fuel spilled out. When they got out in the middle of the Ohio with a swift current, she started to list, so LeClair, an experienced navigator, ran the boat into a mud bank to keep her from sinking. The crew caulked the seams and made all necessary repairs, but the trip up was a series of catastrophes. A log jammed the rudder causing them to hit trees. En route they encountered three storms and the river rose 38 feet. Their average travel time was one mile an hour. Clothes, mattresses and linens were constantly damp and all had a hard time keeping warm.

In the Illinois Canal nearing home base, they could not clear a bridge and had to buy tons of flagstone from a nearby quarry to make the boat ride lower in the water and then had to wait for the water to drop. They were barely able to get through. But at the next bridge, they were not so fortunate, as they had to cut away a part of the exhaust stack with an electric saw.

The crew was weary, cold, miserable and almost sick when they finally arrived at Chicago and pulled into the dock on Ohio Street. But LeClair and staff made her seaworthy again with a good working diesel motor, paddles of heavy oak, new rudders, new coat of paint, new gingerbread, new heating system, washroom facilities, a large recreation room, a bar and wall-to-wall carpeting. She was renamed the *Riverqueen*.

Information for this story supplied from an article in the *Paducah Sun-Democrat* Tuesday, June 4, 1963.

Cyrus Eaton and Strawberries

The West Kentucky Coal Company was a Paducah institution for many years. They transported coal from their west Kentucky mines down the Tradewater and Ohio rivers in company-owned towboats and barges to their unloading tipple at 2nd and Ohio streets, where the coal was unloaded onto conveyors which carried it up to overhead bins.

The first boat I remember was the *Charles E. Richardson*, a large steam paddle boat capable of pushing three loaded barges three abreast. One other vessel, built much later was the *Mark Easton*, a twin-screw diesel boat. Mark Easton of Madisonville, president of West Kentucky Coal, married Alma Davis, who was girl's gym and basketball coach at Augusta Tilghman High School in the late '20s and early '30s. After the Island Creek bought West Kentucky Coal, they had another powerful towboat built and named it for Cyrus Eaton, one of the largest stockholders of Island Creek.

The company decided to bring the *M/V Eaton* to Paducah for its christening and Mr. Eaton notified Ralph Vennum, Paducah manager, and Herbert Richardson, a company official of Paducah, that he planned to fly to Paducah to be here for the christening. Ralph Vennum telephoned Stanley Petter and made him aware of the pending visit, as Vennum knew that the coal company was a substantial customer of Petter Supply.

Mr. Petter bought a magnum of champagne and intended to have it put on the Eaton plane, but two days before the event was scheduled he learned that Eaton was a teetotaler. He changed from champagne to strawberries and had two crates of Dixie Aromas delivered and put aboard the Eaton plane.

A short time later, in August, 1967, Zelma Nicholson and I had decided to marry and several close friends arranged a bachelor party at the Ritz Hotel. Soon after we got started, there was a knock on the door and when the door was opened, I was surprised and pleased to see my boss, Stanley Petter, with that large magnum of champagne. That added to the merriment and before we finished the contents, I gave a toast to Cyrus Eaton for being a teetotaler.

City Hall and Fire Station

Industry Leaders of the Past

The International Shoe Company

The International Shoe Company provided Paducah with a substantial payroll for more than 75 years. How it came here is an interesting story. Former *Paducah Sun-Democrat* feature writer Bob Sanderson, in a 1956 article, said the company was "bribed" into coming to Paducah.

In 1919, Paducah was in dire need of a new industry. Prohibition put an end to the Paducah Brewing Company, the Wallace Vinegar Works and the large distilling industry and its building were idle. One of the largest and most modern was the Friedman-Keiler building on the southeast corner of 2nd and Jefferson. The Paducah Board of Trade, which was the city's chamber of commerce in those days, got in touch with the International Shoe Company in St. Louis about buying the building and converting it into a shoe factory. The shoe company was interested, but not willing to take a chance on a town with no trained shoemakers and where the ability of the people to learn was unknown.

The board of trade went into a huddle. Why not buy the building for the shoe company? If the company would commit to a long-term contract, its payroll advantages to the city would far outweigh the cost of the building. The board submitted the proposition to the public. Did they want an industry badly enough to buy a $100,000 building? They did.

A total of $105,000 was raised and the building was turned over to the shoe company with the understanding that it would belong to the company as soon as it paid out in Paducah wages $20 for every dollar the building cost. International was given 10 years to gain clear title. It paid out in three-and-a-half years.

Paducah received a bonus on the deal, when the company built an addition which doubled the size of the plant and its total employment. By the middle of the century, the company was making an average of 5,760 pairs of shoes a day and making the company's most expensive line of children's shoes. Of 26 plants in the United States and Canada, the Paducah plant ranked fourth. Today, that building and the industry it brought to Paducah is only a memory. That corner, and in fact, the whole block is now a municipal parking lot. International Shoe's building, as have the other buildings on that block - M. Livingston Wholesale Grocers, Paducah Ice Manufacturing Company, Michael Implement Store and the Richmond House - has come and gone.

International Shoe Co. Factory
employing 700 people and producing 1,500,000 pairs of shoes annually

Illinois Central Railroad Shops

I became aware of the shops while I was attending Washington Junior High School, which was prominently situated on the south side of Broadway between 12th and 13th streets. I was 13 and in the eighth grade. The very first morning of school I got there early and sat on the steps on the west side waiting for school to open. Soon another student joined me and told me his name was Rolph Nagel and that he was starting back to school after spending a year in Germany. He said his family was in the tobacco exporting business and still had family in Germany and shipped a lot of tobacco abroad. He said he could speak German, which interested me, for I hadn't met any other youngster who could speak a foreign language or one who traveled abroad. We have been good friends for over 70 years.

The year was 1927 and the Illinois Central Railroad had just begun to build the shops which covered the area from 11th to 16th streets on the south side of Kentucky Avenue. This had been a hollow area and it took several months to fill it with dirt to bring the land up to grade. Giant pile drivers were brought in and many more months went by before all the steel pilings were driven into the earth to stabilize the foundation.

We went to school many days when the air was filled with the incessant pounding noise of the pile drivers. The constant bang-bang-banging was distracting and nerve-wracking, but the teachers and students somehow made it through. Steel construction and erection was still going on when our class moved to the ninth grade at Augusta Tilghman High. We were still within sight and sound of the shops, being on the east and slightly south of the them, but the noise was greatly diminished.

On the northwest corner of 12th and Kentucky was an all-night cafe. Almost 100 percent of the patrons were shop employees. The cafe front, except for a large window, was covered with a white slate-like material, but due to all the smoke and grit from the shops, it was always a dingy gray. In fact, the whole neighborhood was usually coated with a layer of coal dust.

Across the street on the northeast corner facing the cafe, was the 12th Street Garage, which stayed open day and night to accommodate shop people. It was owned and operated by Grover Watkins, a good mechanic who had a number of other auto mechanics in his employ. It was convenient for workers at the shops to park there while at work or to have their cars worked on there. Tom Clark, father of Thomas Earl and Marion Clark, worked at the roundhouse at night and parked his car there. My brother and I ran around in a group that included the Clark children and we got Tommy to borrow his dad's car so we could haul our dates around town. Sometimes Tommy drove his dad to work, took the car and then left it at the garage around midnight and got someone to take him home. Since Harry and I could not always have our dad's car, we double-dated often with Tommy.

Soon after we entered Washington Junior High, the Oehlschlaeger Drugstore moved from the northwest corner of 6th and Broadway to the northwest corner of 12th and Broadway. Horace Green, a pharmacist and long-time employee of Oehlschlaeger's became a partner and the name of the drugstore was changed to G&O. Like all drugstores back then, it had a soda fountain and became a favorite hangout for all the neighborhood school boys. Next door was John Rogers' Grocery, where most of the boys in Washington School ate lunch. We thought their sandwiches, chips, candy bars and Cokes tasted better than the fare in the school lunch room.

During the early days of the shops (1927-1940), a young man named Jimmie Johnson was usually seen hanging around the corner at the drugstore. Jimmie lived on Kentucky Avenue, across the street from the shops, with his parents and sister, Doshia Mae. Jimmie got a job at the shops and after saving a little money, bought a secondhand Maytag washing machine and began washing the soiled overalls of the men at the shops. After he accumulated several hundred dollars, he also began to loan money to some of his fellow workers, many of whom lived paycheck to paycheck. The shop people were paid every other week and many found themselves broke before they got their next pay. So they borrowed $5 or $10 from Jimmie. He charged interest of $1 a week for $5 or $2 for $10. Every week the loan was not repaid, the same interest was added. So if you borrowed $5 and didn't pay for five weeks, you owed him $10. Jimmie would be found in the doorway at the drugstore every payday, loaning and collecting money.

Eventually, he quit the shops, went into the loan business and also became a bondsman. Just before he died he had a "lock" on all the business of bonding people at the city and county courts. At his death, he had extensive real estate holdings.

Several years before World War II began, my brother Harry went to work in the boiler room at the IC shops. His job was "bucking" rivets. Harry was inside a locomotive boiler shell with a bucking tool while the boiler maker was on the outside with his air ham-

Industry in Paducah

mer driving the rivet in place. It was hard, hot, noisy and dirty work and when Harry got off he was covered head to foot with grit and grime. He was on the swing shift, working from 4 p.m. to midnight. Since I was off from work at 5 p.m. and we had only one car in the family, I picked him up after he got off work. Usually I would have been out on a date and dressed up, and he was dirty and tired. It made me feel bad and guilty that my lot was so much better than his.

The Illinois Central was a very good customer of Petter Supply, although the company purchasing office in Chicago did most of the buying and regularly put out lists for bids, and we didn't land many of the big orders. We did a nice business on their pick-up needs, which were no small item. When I was on the local delivery truck, I made trips to the IC almost every day. I delivered orders to their storeroom, which was a large brick building right behind the long building that faced Kentucky. The storekeeper, Frank Erdman, and I became good friends.

During that period, my sisters, Ruth and Edna, were both married and living in Chicago. We visited them once or twice a year, usually at Thanksgiving or Christmas. Unless it was during a vacation, I would ask and get an extra day off so I could stay longer. Once when I arranged for a trip to Chicago, Mr. Petter suggested I take an extra day and make a few business calls on customers whose main offices were in Chicago. One of these was the Illinois Central. I was asked to call on Leonard King, vice president and purchasing agent. I made the call just before noon and was given a very nice reception by Mr. King. He had known Stanley Petter for years and said they were close friends. While we were discussing business, we heard music from a band marching down the street below. Mr. King explained that the American Legion was holding a convention at the Sherman Hotel just down the street and that he was invited to sit with President Harry Truman, the main speaker. He said, "No, I'm not going. In fact, I wouldn't walk across the street to see that S.O.B." It was apparent he was not a Truman man.

Paducah's Oldest Industry
Paducah Marine Ways

Paducah Marine Ways was Paducah's oldest industry, dating back to 1843. That year, the city contracted with Elijah Murray of St. Louis for the right to use his patent for construction of a marine railroad here. Murray agreed and received $1,000 for his patent and $500 for supervising construction of the Ways along the bank of the Tennessee River at Washington Street.

The marine railway is a device for removing large boats from

the river to make hull repairs. It was also used to launch steamboats and such river craft built in the Paducah yards. It was the forerunner of the dry dock, which replaced it. The railway consisted of a series of cradles which ran on inclined tracks from a point below the water's edge to a point halfway up the river bank. Boats floated into position over the submerged cradles which ran on incline tracks and onto the bank as the cradles moved up the inclined rails. Steel cables attached to huge windlasses pulled the cradles upward. The windlasses were turned by a powerful steam engine.

The city leased the Ways to a private concern and in 1853 it was discovered that the railway was in bad shape. The cradles were careened, the logs sunken and the bank washed away. The city took over the concern and advertised for bids for construction of a new railway, to be copied after one in operation in Madison, Ind.

Elijah Murray was the successful bidder and was awarded the contract to build a Ways with eight sections and the capacity and power to draw from the river boats and vessels measuring up to 350 feet. The new Ways was completed in 1854, leased to the Watts and Givens Company with Murray in charge of operations. The old Ways is pictured in several history books at the Paducah Public

Paducah Marine Ways, 1900s
Above and opposite

Library. One in particular shows four paddle wheelers pulled upon the railway onto dry ground and being repaired at the same time.

The rebuilt Ways continued to operate for many years and has had several changes of ownership since its beginning. During many of the years I worked at Petter Supply, which was two blocks north of the Ways, the company was operated by the Ayer & Lord Tie Division of the Koppers Company, which also bought, processed and creosoted telephone poles and railroad ties in their yards in Brookport and Carbondale, Ill. Guy P. Holland was the manager.

Howard Twitchell, who was a football star at Tilghman High School when Joe Clifton played, was a caulker in 1926, became an iron worker and later was bookkeeper for many years at the Ways, until the company transferred him to the tie plant in Carbondale. Howard's father, Jacob, was a timekeeper in the Ways in the early 1900s. Howard's younger brother, Paul, worked there part time as a painter.

Paducah Brewery
City Consumers Company

The Paducah Brewery Company was organized in 1900 by Harry and Abraham Livingston, John W. Keiler and F.W. Katterjohn, all Paducah residents who had other business interests here. They erected an impressive brick and concrete five-story building along the railroad tracks at 10th and Monroe, with Katterjohn, a brick maker and contractor, in charge of the construction.

In 1909, they hired expert brew master Charles Gustav Vahlkamp, a St. Louis native of German descent, to manage the company. (The Vahlkamps lived at 121 Fountain Ave. and were my next door neighbors when I lived on Fountain from 1933 to 1940.) Under the capable management of Vahlkamp, the brewery advanced the name of Paducah over a widespread area, with their products, Paducah Pilsner and Paduka Beer. The advent of Prohibition in 1919 forced the closing of this prosperous company and the building became a liability for its owners.

In 1920, seven members of the company, Charles, Henry and Al Vahlkamp; Harry and Abe Livingston; John W. Keiler; and F.W. Katterjohn, got together and organized the City Consumers Company. They bought all their raw milk products from producers in the west Kentucky area and sold their processed products, milk, butter, ice cream and other dairy foods, throughout western Kentucky, west Tennessee and southern Illinois. A large fleet of wagons and trucks made daily house-to-house deliveries to residences, grocers and commercial establishments. Many area farmers converted from tobacco production to dairy farming, to supply the needs of their trade. The company advertised under the name Goldbloom Milk.

It grew from 40 employees to an industry that employed 135

in 1945. That year, the company was sold to the Midwest Dairy Company, which continued to operate the plant until recent times. Today, all that remains at the site is a 60-foot-high brick smokestack, a landmark of what was at the time a major Paducah industry. Like City Consumers, other smaller dairy plants in Paducah, namely Miller, Dexter, Rector and Dudley dairies, gradually disappeared from the scene. All three of the Vahlkamp men have died. Only Mrs. Al Vahlkamp survives and is presently living in the old Vahlkamp home on Fountain Avenue.

Paducah Brewery

Worthy Manufacturing
M. Fine Company

The Depression of the 1930s hit Paducah hard. Factories were closed or on shortened schedules and unemployment was high. The Paducah Board of Trade, headed by Leo F. Keiler, ran across Worthy Manufacturing, a Chicago company interested in locating a new 700-employee shirt-making factory in the South. The board of trade asked if Worthy would be interested in a proposition similar to the one accepted by International Shoe in the early 1920s. At that time, the board bought the Friedman-Keiler building at 2nd and Jefferson and negotiated a contract with the shoe company which resulted in its coming to Paducah. Worthy was interested, but no existing suitable building could be found in Paducah. Nor could public contributions be counted on to raise the funds to build or buy a building if one were located. Jobs were scarce and people just didn't have the money to give.

The board finally decided to build the Worthy Company a building to its specifications and to finance it through an ingenious scrip stamp plan. The plan never was popular and almost ended in disaster. But it laid the groundwork to furnish employment to up to 400 persons in Paducah.

This is the way the scrip stamp plan worked: paper certificates about the size of official paper money were redeemable in cash only after the required number of stamps had been affixed. This scrip was issued in denominations of $1, $5, $10 and $20. On the back of each certificate was a space for the stamps to be affixed. They were sold to merchants, storekeepers, banks, employees and everyone else who agreed to accept scrip as legal tender. That was about everybody in Paducah.

On a $1 certificate, the person who passed it first had to pay one cent. The second person paid two cents, the third three or four cents. Then the certificate could be redeemed for $1 in cash. It was through the sale of the stamps that the board of trade raised the money for the factory building.

The board raised $75,000 in this way and had the building erected on the southwest corner of 8th and Burnett. The Worthy Company began operations in 1932 and all went well for three years. Then the company went broke and the building stood idle. The scrip which had been issued to pay for the plant was still in circulation and was getting more unpopular by the day. Workers received half their pay in cash and the other half in Paducah scrip. The paper certificates disappeared after the 1937 flood. The Worthy Company went bankrupt before it had paid out enough in wages to acquire title to the building.

The board of trade contacted Isadore Fine, who was operating similar factories in New Albany and Jeffersonville, Ind. He agreed to move one or both of his factories here under the same proposition offered Worthy. The transfer was made in 1935. David Fine moved to Paducah as manager. By the mid-1950s, M. Fine & Co. had an annual payroll of $800,000. Its 350, mostly women, employees turned out an average of 300 dozen men's work shirts per day, which were sold throughout the United states. In 1941, the M. Fine Company acquired a clear title to the building after paying out approximately $2 million in wages.

Worthy Manufacturing Co. - M. Fine Co.

Southern Textile Machinery Company

For many years, the Southern Textile Machinery Company was a very active firm, providing Paducah with a good payroll for a number of people. It was organized in 1906 to manufacture an attachment invented by E.O. Davis of Paducah, which improved the efficiency of hosiery looping machines. Looping machines are sewing machines used to close the toes of seamless hosiery. Davis worked for the old Paducah Hosiery Mills, which later became the Priester Hosiery Mill at 9th and Kentucky. He conceived the idea of substituting a lock stitch for the chain stitch used on the early German machines mainly used by the hosiery industry. The German chain stitch had no elasticity, which caused hosiery to unravel completely when one thread was broken.

After some small success with the Davis attachment, officials located William Carpenter Wright of Cleveland, Ohio, who found a way to make the lock stitch work with a smooth revolving motion instead of the jerky ratchet action originally employed. Southern Textile bought the Wright patent and combined it with the Davis attachment and in 1910, set up a corporation to manufacture a looping machine which contained the good features of both inventions. The officials of the corporation were Richard Rudy, president; E.O. Davis, vice president; William F. Paxton, secretary-treasurer; Finis E. Lack Sr.; F.W. Katterjohn; James P. Smith; and H.F. Drink. Davis received shares of stock in payment for his invention and after a short period, sold his interest back to other shareholders. Rudy resigned a year later and Finis Lack was elevated to the presidency.

When the United States slapped an embargo on the importation of German-made products because of that country's blockade of the British Isles in World War I, the Southern Textile Company began to flourish. George Flournoy became president and sales manager, while W.P. Paxton was in charge of production. Paxton's original salary was $15 a week, plus a stipulated amount of company stock. In 1921, the Citizen's Bank fell heir to a building at 3rd and Norton and since both Flournoy and Paxton held interests in Citizen's, the site became available for Southern Textile.

Flournoy, who steered the company through some of its roughest years, served as president until his death in 1927. William Percy Paxton became president. Paxton had been an office manager for the E.E. Sutherland Drug Company since 1908. He became active in Southern Textile in 1914. The company continued to grow and do well. In 1948, it employed 131 people and by 1956, it had grown to 281 employees. The new hosiery looper process used by Southern Textile became the standard in the industry and was used worldwide. So did the outer-garment looper developed in the Paducah plant and marketed in 1949. The outer-garment looper did away with finishing sweaters and similar garments by hand.

In 1953, Southern Textile put on the market for the first time an automatic hosiery testing machine developed in the Paducah plant. It enabled a tester to inspect 200 dozen pairs of stockings in an eight-hour day, where formerly only 80 dozen a day was possible.

Upon the death in 1952 of William P. Paxton, his son, Tomas Paxton, became president, his brother, William F. Paxton, vice president and secretary and F.S. Lack, treasurer.

Tomas A. Paxton died April 26, 1984, and his younger brother, William Perce Paxton II, became owner and manager. Although Southern Textile is no longer at the old location at 3rd and Norton, it continues to supply equipment and parts for the hosiery industry from its plant on Highway 60 west of Paducah.

Claussner Hosiery Company

*I*n 1921, all but five percent of U.S. hosiery was made in the New England and northern states. George Flournoy and William P. Paxton, officers of the Southern Textile Company of Paducah, makers of hosiery knitting machines, visited the New England mills to study their manufacturing operations with the idea of operating a hosiery mill in Paducah. But the eastern mill owners laughed at the idea of trying to operate a mill so far south, indicating that hosiery knitting was a trade which required great skill. They said "Kentucky hillbillies" could never be taught how to make silk stockings. The Paducah men knew better because of their experiences at Southern Textile. But they knew they had to get someone who knew more about the manufacture of hosiery than they. When they found Bob Claussner, who had been with the Wayne Knitting Mill in New York, they knew they had found their man.

By offering Claussner a salary and an interest in the hosiery firm, they organized the hosiery company in 1921. Claussner was made production manager. They started production with 16 workers and four machines. Sales for the first year were about $50,000. By October of 1942, volume was $2 million, with 600 employees in three plants. Annual payroll amounted to $650,000.

As Germany was the dominant country in the hosiery industry, the company was named for Claussner, who was born in Elbeneburg, Germany, hoping this name would enhance its image and make its acceptance easier. Claussner retired in 1937 and died in California in 1941. His son, Bob Jr., joined the hosiery company in 1925 and when he retired in 1967, was executive vice president and general manager. He died in 1989.

Claussner made full-fashion and seamless nylon hose and sold in every state in the union. One of their plants did custom "thread throwing" (twisting) for other hosiery mills. Their seamless division, which at the time was newly-created, was introduced to meet the demand for this type of hose. Claussner's affiliate, Marvel Manufacturing, made a device to repair nylon hosiery that was sold or leased to foreign countries.

I knew many of the boys who became knitters at Claussner. Among them were Jack House, Jess Crocker, Morris McBride, Harry Mathis and Albert Otto. They were paid on a piece-work basis and permitted to work many hours overtime. Many earned over $300 a week. Claussner's main building at 2800 Adams still stands, but Claussner is no longer in business. The hosiery business which once thrived here and provided Paducah with the highest pay wage in town and offered a substantial payroll for many people, is but a memory of the past.

Industries Lost to Paducah

From the rosy and promising picture painted in 1956, our centennial year, look at what has happened since. Of the once growing number of about 20 industries in existence, about 12 have gone out of business. The old Illinois Central Railroad shops, now VMV, has a force a third of its former peak and the Lockheed-Martin (formerly Martin Marietta) plant faces an uncertain future. This is about 4,000 jobs lost since then.

And where we used to produce much of our own products locally, many local providers are out of business. Most of our many former local dairies, bakeries, butchers and produce growers are gone and no longer serve our area. I anguish over every lost industry and hope we will be able to attract more. And it puzzles me that all over our area, building is booming and we seem to be prosperous with new retail stores and service establishments springing up on all sides. I wonder what engine is driving this growth? Of course, it is great to see and I hope it continues. I credit our emphasis on travel and tourist promotion and the marine industry for a large part of the health of the region.

Paducah Water Plant

BIBLIOGRAPHY & PHOTO CREDITS

Directories, City of Paducah, 1882 to present.

Fairhurst, Richard E. *The Fairhurst Essays: A Public Look
    at a Private Memoir.* The Patric Press, 1980.

Lesslie, Donald E. *Paducah Gateway, A History of Railroads
    in Western Kentucky.* Troll Publishing, 1978.

Neuman, Fred. *The Story of Paducah.* Young Printing, Paducah,
    1927, revised by Catherine Neuman Adams.
    Image Graphics, 1979.

Purcell, Martha Grassham. *Stories of Old Kentucky.*
    American Book Co., 1915.

Paducah Evening Sun

The Paducah News Democrat

The Paducah Sun-Democrat

The Paducah Sun

The Paducah Public Library, Microfilm and Microfish

Robertson, John E.L. *Paducah 1830-1980,
    A Sessquicentennial History.* Image Graphics, 1980.

Dortch, Nat; White, Barron; Fairhurst, Richard E.
    Rotary Club of Paducah. Leake Printing, 1980.

Wells, Camille. *Architecture of Paducah and McCracken County,*
    Image Graphics, 1981.

Marshall County Genealogical Society.
    History of Marshall County, KY, Benton, KY ,Reprint 1993.

Massac County, Illinois History. Turner Publishing Co., 1987.

Market House Museum.

Paducah Community College Library.

Mrs. Joy Walden of Lamon Furniture & Antiques.

W.L. "Dub" Beasley.